SHAKE UP
SCIENCE 3

Pearson Education Limited
Edinburgh Gate
Harlow
Essex CM20 2JE
England
and Associated Companies throughout the world.

www.pearsonelt.com

© Pearson Education Limited 2016

All rights reserved; no part of this publication may be reproduced, stored in a retrieval system, or transmitted in any form or by any means, electronic, mechanical, photocopying, recording, or otherwise without the prior written permission of the Publishers.

First published 2016
ISBN: 978-1-2921-4477-1

Set in AdProLTStd, AgilitaLTPro, ArtaStd, BradleyHand, FuturaLTPro, GillSansInfantStd, MemphisLTCYR, MorrisFreestyleStd, VAGRoundedLTPro, VAGRoundedStd, ZapfDingbatsStd, ZemkeHandITCStd

Authorized Adaptation from the U.S. English Language Edition, entitled Interactive Science, Copyright © 2012 by Pearson Education, Inc. or its affiliates. Used by permission. All Rights Reserved.

Pearson and Scott Foresman are trademarks, in the US and/or other countries, of Pearson Education, Inc. or its affiliates.

This publication is protected by copyright, and prior to any prohibited reproduction, storage in a retrieval system, or transmission by any for or by any means, electronic, mechanical, photocopying, recording or likewise, permission should be obtained from International Rights Sales, 221 River Street, Hoboken, NJ 07030 U.S.A

This book is authorized for sale worldwide.

Acknowledgements
Picture credits
The publisher would like to thank the following for their kind permission to reproduce their photographs:

(Key: b-bottom; c-centre; l-left; r-right; t-top)

123RF.com: 29/1 (a), 30/4, 32 (d), 34cl, 38/6, 40/6, 46/2, 64/1, Yuri Bizgajmer 17t/2, 72/8, Mr.Smith Chetanachan 17b/1, Chiyacat 15/3, Steven Coling 85b, Steve Collender 67, Oleg Doroshenko 38/5, 55/7, ermess 43/4, Ben Goode 56/2, 83 (Unit 7), Roman Gorielov 55/6, heinteh 15/2, Steve Hutchinson 82 (Unit 3), Andrea Izzotti 22/2, 23b, Sergey Jarochkin 68r/4, joruba 60/1, khunaspix 17t/3, Dusan Kostic 76/3, lucadp 43t/1, 55/4, 83 (Unit 9), Auttapon Moonsawad 17b/4, Nikkytok 8br, ronen 17t/6, Weldon Schloneger 10c, 29/2 (b), solomonjee 12/6, 17t/4, Anton Starikov 68/2, strannikfox 10tr, Oksana Tkachuk 68/1, tobkatrina 72/1, wernerimages 75/4; **Alamy** 72/7, National Geographic Creative 77/4, Nordicphotos 71t, Onoky / Photononstop 47, Catalin Petolea 36, Dmytro Skorobogatov 71b, Stockchildren 19bc, Stocktrek Images, Inc 51t, Travelibuk 65; **Corbis:** 68 / Ocean 73l; **Fotolia.com:** Ad_Hominem 50/4, 51cl, 51bl, 51br, ALCE 55/2, Anrymos 8t, Antonsov85 15/4, Ask-Fotografie 48/5, Baibaz 68/3, Mikkel Bigandt 44, Blackzheep 14l, Butsaya12 51cr, Sergiy Bykhunenko 6/2, 82 (Unit 1), Steve Byland 19t/3, Tony Campbell 27t, Danimarco 38/4, 40/1, DenisNata 4t/3, Destillat 82 (Unit 5), Biletskiy Evgeniy 57, F9photos 20/3, Elisabetta Figus 4t/4, 28l/7, Fuchsphotography 72/6, Funkenzauber 40/3, Galam 60/2, 80/7, Gekaskr 4t/5, 28r/2, Gertrudda 20/2, 28r/3, Budimir Jevtic 5, Pavel Klimenko 40/2, 55/5, Igor Mojzes 40/4, Mouse_Md 56/3, 80/6, Nata777_7 20/1, Okea 24, 28r/11, Popova Olga 15/1, Ollirg 11b, Oneinchpunch 29/1 (b), Pakhnyushchyy 38/1, 40/7, Ruth P. Peterkin 55/8, Pixindy 40/5, Alexander Potapov 20 (Coral), Procy_Ab 50/1, Pyty 10tl, Goce Risteski 19br, Rohappy 48/1, Rxr3rxr3 20 (Deer), Carlos André Santos 82 (Unit 2), Scenery1 80/5, Sondem 56/1, Studiodr 20 (Cactus), Sunny studio 4t/1, 6/3, 28r/1, Viperagp 60/4, 80/2, Aleksandr Volkov 10b, 28l/10, 29/2 (a), Voyagerix 38/2, WavebreakmediaMicro 4t/2, 28l/1, Chris White 63t, 72/4, Krzysztof Wiktor 26bl, 29/2 (c), Wildnerdpix 38/3, 40/8, Xixinxing 13/4, Oleg Zhukov 26br, 28l/5; **Getty Images:** Creatas / Dynamic Graphics 13/2, danmitchell 87t, Kjerstin Gjengeda 62, iStock 19bl, Stock4b-Rf 73r, The Image Bank / Chip Simons 13/3; **Pearson Education Ltd:** Studio 8 55/1, Tudor Photography 68l/4; **PhotoDisc:** C. McIntyre 25tc; **Shutterstock.com:** 2xSamara.com 33, 77/3, 28r/8, Africa Studio 75/3, Rainer Albiez 30/2, 32 (c), 34l, Balazs Kovacs Images 63b, 80/4, Nadezhda Bolotina 11t, Tyler Boyes 10t, 29/2 (d), Brocreative 12/1, 28r/6, P. Burghardt 76/5, Steve Byland 20 (Alligator), David Carillet 50/5, ChameleonsEye 43/2, Cheryl E. Davis 11c, Ana de Sousa 76/4, design56 87bl, Dja65 64/3, Iakov Filimonov 74, focal point 14r, Fotokostic 77/1, Natali Glado 72/3, Dee Golden 66, Tom Gowanlock 14cr, Mat Hayward 6/1, Ramona Heim 77/2, Brian Hendricks 17t/1, 29/3 (c), Stuart Jenner 30/3, 32 (b), 34r, Matt Jeppson 22/1, 29/1 (c), Jtairat 13/1, Junne 68 (b), Jason Kasumovic 19t/4, Kathy Kay 22/3, Luis Louro 76/1, Rudolf MadÃ¡r 25tr, Don Mammoser 19t/1, 22/4, Andrew McDonough 17b/2, 28l/9, michaeljung 30/1, 32 (a), 34cr, Stefanie Mohr Photography 64/2, monticello 68 (d), Mr.Joe 64/4, Aksenova Natalya 72/5, Dmitry Naumov 72/2, Cristina Negoita 12/5, newphotoservice 4b/1, nienora 46/3, Nitr 68 (a), Noerenberg 17b/3, Khoroshunova Olga 49, Denis and Yulia Pogostins 14cl, Praisaeng 60/3, 80/1, Lawrence Roberg 76/2, Dulce Rubia 12/4, 28l/4, 29/3 (a), Ruta Production 13t, Nicram Sabod 19t/2, 23t, 29/1 (d), Galushko Sergey 75/1, Maciej Sojka 46/1, 52, 53, 55bl, 55br, Stihii 35 (a), 35 (b), Dan Tautan 80/3, Timmary 12/2, Toa55 43/3, 55/3, 85t, Camilo Torres 68 (c), Vinicius Tupinamba 8bl, Symonenko Viktoriia 70, Vikulin 75/2, visionaryft 82 (Unit 4), Wavebreak Premium 4b/2, Brian C. Weed 12/3, 17t/5, 29/3 (d), xfox01 46/4, 82 (Unit 6), Yanas 29/3 (b), Shukaylova Zinaida 50/2, 50/3, Peter Zvonar 58

All other images © Pearson Education

Cover photo © *Front:* **Getty Images:** Kristian Sekulic r; **Shutterstock.com:** fivespots l; *Back:* **Fotolia.com:** f9photos c; **Shutterstock.com:** Jim Lozouski r, Nicram Sabod l

Contents

Unit 1 The Nature of Science 4
  What is science?

Unit 2 Technology and Tools 12
  How do people solve problems?

Unit 3 Plants and Animals 20
  How do plants and animals live in their habitats?

Review 1–3 28

Unit 4 Body and Growth 30
  How do we grow and change?

Unit 5 Earth's Materials 38
  What is Earth made of?

Unit 6 The Solar System 46
  What are the sun, moon, and planets like?

Review 4–6 54

Unit 7 Weather 56
  How does weather change over time?

Unit 8 Matter 64
  What is matter?

Unit 9 Energy, Motion, and Force 72
  How do energy and forces make objects move?

Review 7–9 80

Skills 82

Unit 1 The Nature of Science

What is science?

1 What senses do we have? Look and match.

| 1 | 2 | 3 | 4 | 5 |

(hearing) (taste) (smell) (touch) (sight)

2 What do you use the different parts of your body for? Read and write.

1 smell   _nose_   **a** ears

2 taste   _____   **b** mouth

3 sight   _____   **c** ~~nose~~

4 touch   _____   **d** eyes

5 hearing   _____   **e** hands

3 Which senses do you use in each activity? Look and mark (✓).

	smell	sight	taste	hearing	touch
1	✓				
2					

4 Unit 1

4 How do our senses help us to find out about the world? Read and write the five senses.

Reading Tip

Read the text and underline the body parts. This will help you choose the correct senses.

Saturday, September 12

I am in my grandmother's garden. It is very pretty. My grandmother's (**1**) ___sight___ isn't very good, but she uses her other senses. There are a lot of big apple trees and she uses her hands for (**2**) _____. When she eats the apples from the trees, she uses her mouth for (**3**) _____. She uses her ears for (**4**) _____ the birds in the trees. There are flowers next to the trees. She uses her nose for (**5**) _____.

5 Look at 4. Read and match.

1 hearing — c
2 smell   a apple trees
3 touch   b apples
4 taste   c birds
5 sight   d garden
                   e flowers

6 How do you use your senses? Complete for you.

1 I use my ears for _hearing. I hear an airplane._

2 _____ smell. _____

3 _____ touch. _____

4 _____ taste. _____

5 _____ sight. _____

Unit 1 5

Lesson 1 • What kinds of skills do scientists use?

1 What do we do in science? Look and write.

~~observe~~   predict   senses   results   experiment

1. observe
2. _____
3. _____
4. _____
5. _____

2 Mike has to do an experiment for homework. Read and write. Use the words from 1.

Hi Luke,

How are you? I have lots of homework this week ☹.

Our science teacher, Mr. Burton, wants us to carry out a(n) **(1)** _experiment_ at home.

Mr. Burton wants us to ask a question and then do an experiment to find out the answer. First, he wants us to **(2)** _____ the answer. That's difficult! He says we can then compare our answer with the **(3)** _____ at the end.

He thinks the best way to **(4)** _____ is to use our **(5)** _____, like sight, smell, taste, touch, and hearing.

Help! What experiment can I do?

Write back soon!

Mike

6   Unit 1

3 Look at **2**. Which are the simple present verbs? Underline.

Grammar Tip

We **have** five senses: smell, hearing, touch, sight, and taste.

4 Mike wrote the results of his experiment. Complete the sentences.

Mike's Experiment

Question: Do the birds like Tree A or Tree B more?

I predict that the birds like Tree A more.

Birds in Tree A and Tree B between 3:00 P.M. and 4:00 P.M.:

	Tree A	Tree B
Monday	5	4
Tuesday	3	4
Wednesday	1	1
Thursday	2	2
Friday	6	3

1 It's Monday. Tree A __has__ five birds and Tree B _____ four birds.

2 It's Tuesday. Tree A _____ three birds and Tree B _____ four birds.

3 It's Wednesday. Tree A and Tree B _____ one bird.

4 It's Thursday. Tree A _____ and _____.

5 It's Friday. _____.

5 Mike predicted that the birds like Tree A more. Is he correct? Circle.

Y / N

Unit 1 7

Lesson 2 • How do scientists find answers?

1 Simon investigates how seeds grow. Read and write.

height   conclusion   measurement   hypothesis   investigate

Simon's Science Blog   Posted: September 5th

Today, I am doing an experiment. I want to (1) _investigate_ if seeds need water to grow. First, I ask the question: Do seeds need water to grow? Then, before I do the experiment, I need to make a (2) _____ to answer the question. I predict that the seeds that are watered will grow.

Now, I need to plan a fair test: I put seeds in two pots. Each day, I water only one pot. Then I look each day to see which seeds grow into a plant. I want to record the (3) _____ of the plants, so I take a (4) _____ every day.

Then I do the same experiment again to see if the results are the same.

Posted: September 21st

I finish my repeat experiment today. I compare results and draw my (5) _____. Seeds need water to grow. My hypothesis is correct ☺.

2 Write the details of Simon's experiment. Use the underlined text in 1.

1 Ask the question: _Do seeds need water to grow?_

2 Hypothesis: _____

3 Fair test: _____

4 Repeat the investigation: _____

5 Conclusion: _____

8 Unit 1

③ Look at 1 and find *First* and *Then*. Circle.

④ Simon is planning another experiment. Read and write the steps of the experiment.

Grammar Tip

First, they ask questions.
Then they investigate.

Hypothesis   Conclusion   ~~Question~~   Fair test   Repeat

Question : Do plants need the sun to grow?

_____ : I predict that the plant in the sun will grow.

_____ : I put one plant in the sun and I put one plant in the dark. I measure the height of each plant each day.

_____ : I do the experiment again. I take measurements.

_____ : Plants need the sun to grow.

⑤ Write the experiment in Simon's blog.

Posted: September 25th

I want to _investigate_ if plants need the sun to grow. First, I ask the question: _____? Then I need to make _____ _____ to answer the question: _____ _____. Now, I need to plan a _____.
This is my test: _____.
I take _____. I measure the _____ of the plants every day. Then I repeat the _____. I compare results and draw my _____.

Unit 1 9

Lesson 3 • How do scientists collect and share data?

1 **Can you describe these rocks? Look, circle, and write.**

thy(rough)cbsmoothsharpdjwroundedeopjaggedfnulargetsmalltall

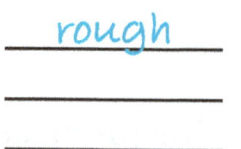

rough

_____

2 **We use our senses to find out how the rocks are different. Look and circle.**

1 The (basalt) / pumice is smooth. **Basalt**

2 The pumice / granite is large.

3 The pumice / granite is rounded. **Pumice**

4 The basalt / granite is rough. **Granite**

3 **Look at 1 and 2. Write about the rocks.**

Scientists use different senses to collect (**1**) _data_ about the rocks. They use their senses of sight and touch to observe and measure the rocks. The results are very different. (**2**) _____ is a smooth rock. (**3**) _____ is large and rough. (**4**) _____ is rough and rounded.

10 Unit 1

4 Look at the photos and the height of the trees. Complete the bar chart.

Fir tree — Fir = 80 m

Oak tree — Oak = 40 m

Olive tree — Olive = 7 m

Reading Tip

Tables, charts, and graphs help us understand a lot of information quickly. They can help us to compare things.

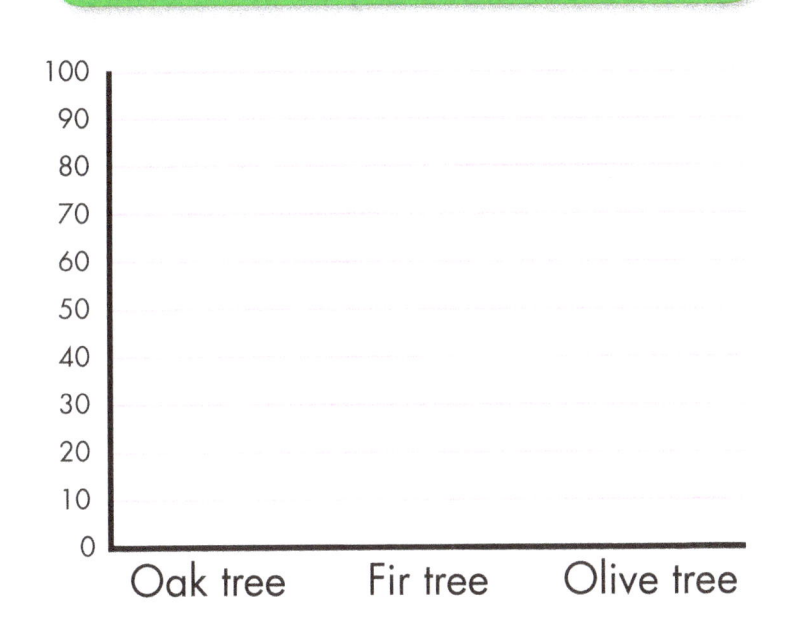

5 Look at 4. Complete the chart. Then write the answers.

	Oak Tree	Fir Tree	Olive Tree
Where?	England	North America	Mediterranean
Height?			
Leaves?	smooth	very sharp	sharp

1 It's from North America. _____

2 It's 40 meters high. _____

3 Its leaves are very sharp. _____

6 Look at 5. Which is your favorite tree? Write.

My favorite tree is a _____ tree. It's from _____.
It's _____ high. Its leaves _____.

Unit 1   11

Unit 2 Technology and Tools

How do people solve problems?

1 Do you have any of these objects at home? Look and match.

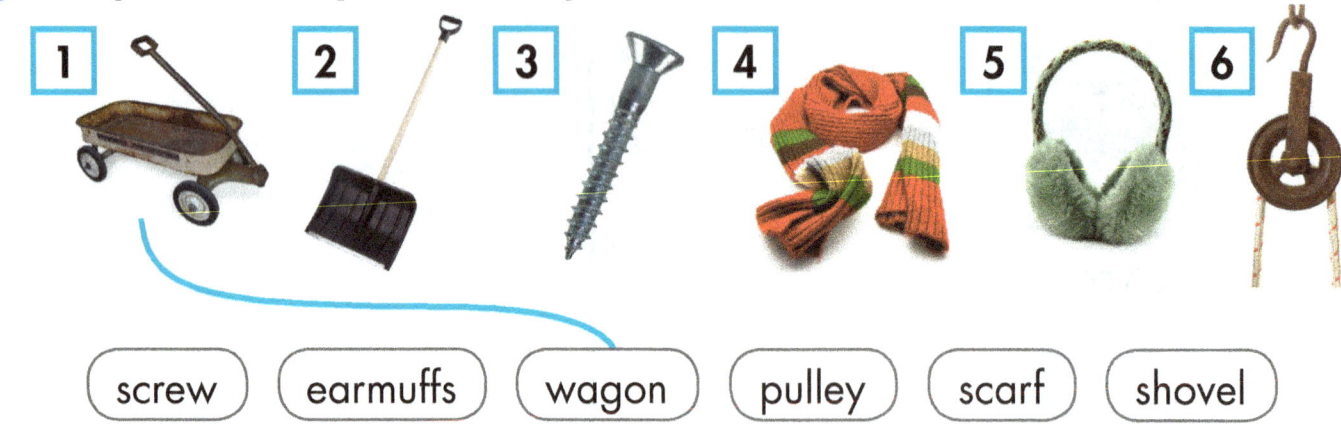

1 2 3 4 5 6

screw   earmuffs   wagon   pulley   scarf   shovel

2 When do you use the objects? Read. Circle *T* (true) or *F* (false).

1 I wear my scarf when it's cold. — **T** / F

2 I wear my earmuffs when it's hot. — T / F

3 I use my shovel when it snows. — T / F

4 I use the wagon when my bags are light. — T / F

5 I use a screw when I want to hold things together. — T / F

3 What do you use? Read and write. Use the words from 1.

1 When my ears are cold, I use _earmuffs_.

2 When there's a lot of snow, I use a _____.

3 When I need to lift a very heavy bucket, I use a _____.

4 When it's windy, I wear a _____.

4 Learn how to build a treehouse. Read and write. (The steps are in the wrong order.)

~~screws~~   wagon   earmuffs
scarf   shovel   pulley

HOW TO BUILD A TREEHOUSE!

☐ [A] Use (**1**) __screws__ to put the wood together. Now it looks like a house!

☐ [B] Use a (**2**) _____ to lift it up the tree.

☐ [C] First, use a (**3**) _____ to pull the wood to the tree. The wood is heavy.

☐ [D] Remember! If it's cold, wear (**4**) _____ on your ears and a (**5**) _____!

☐ [E] Then cut the wood with a saw. Use a (**6**) _____ to move the small bits of wood you don't need from the yard.

Reading Tip
Look at the words on either side of the gap to help you decide which word to choose. If it's a noun, decide if it's singular or plural.

5 Look at **4**. Put the sentences in the correct order.

6 What do you use? Look and write.

1 When I open the curtains, I use a __pulley.__

2 When I'm at the beach, I _____.

3 _____

4 _____

Unit 2   13

Lesson 1 • How do people design new things?

1 Read this online clothes forum. Circle.

FASHION FIRST!

I ♥ clothes: Do you have a question about clothes? What's your (1) material / *goal*? Do you want to know what (2) material / goal to wear? I can help you!

Becks202: Hi! I like walking in the winter. I need a jacket that's (3) hard / light so I can move easily.

I ♥ clothes: Buy a fleece jacket. It isn't (4) soft / heavy. Also, it doesn't make you very hot or very cold.

Jules909: Hi! I'm going to a party. I love dancing, but I don't want to get hot. What dress can I wear?

I ♥ clothes: Wear a cotton dress. It's (5) heavy / light and (6) soft / hard.

Jules909: Thanks! I'm really excited about the party now!

2 Which kinds of material can these clothes be made of? Think and mark (✓).

	cotton	corduroy	fleece	rubber
pants	✓	✓		
boots				
dress				
sweater				
hat				

3 Can you describe the items of clothing? Look and write.

Grammar Tip

Fleece is a **soft** material.
Rubber is a **hard** material.

1 My pants are ____heavy____. 2 My blouse is _____.

3 My sweater is _____. 4 My shoes are _____.

4 What material are the items of clothing in 3 made of? Write.

| fleece | cotton | ~~corduroy~~ | rubber |

1 They're ____corduroy.____ 2 It's _____.

3 _____ 4 _____

5 Write about your clothes. Use the words in the box.

| fleece | dress | corduroy | shoes |
| pants | cotton | shirt | rubber | skirt |

1 My _pants are light. They're cotton._____

2 My _____. It's / They're _____.

3 My _____. _____

4 My _____. _____

Unit 2   15

6 What items of clothing and materials are good in different seasons? Sort and write.

Items of Clothing

~~gloves~~   hat   dress
boots   jacket   pants
shirt   shoes   skirt

Materials

fleece   cotton
corduroy   rubber   light
heavy   soft   hard

gloves

Winter   Summer

7 What is the best design for each item of clothing? Read and write.

1 I wear boots when it's raining. They're heavy. They're ___rubber___ (fleece / rubber).

2 I wear a shirt when it's hot. It's cotton. It's _____ (hard / soft).

3 I wear pants when it's hot. They're _____ (rubber / cotton).

4 I wear corduroy when it's cold. It's _____ (heavy / light).

8 Write about the clothes you wear.

1 (cold) *I wear a jacket when it's cold.* It's heavy. It's corduroy.

2 (raining) _____

3 (snowing) _____

4 (hot) _____

16   Unit 2

Lesson 2 · How do we use tools and machines?

1 All the photos show machines. Mark (✓) the simple machines.

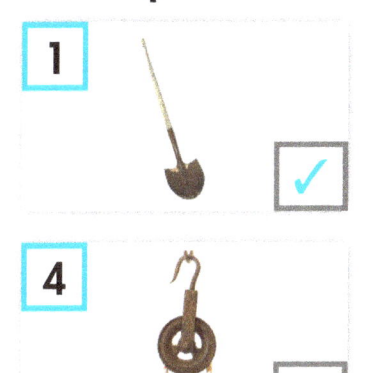

1. ✓
2. ☐
3. ☐
4. ☐
5. ☐
6. ☐

2 What simple machine do the photos show? Circle.

1 lever / **(inclined plane)**
2 pulley / wedge
3 lever / wedge
4 levers / inclined plane

3 Match the descriptions and the words. Write.

| inclined plane | lever | wedge | ~~pulley~~ | simple machine |

1 It moves an object sideways. _____pulley_____

2 It moves things. An example is a shovel. _____

3 It pushes things apart. _____

4 You use it to move a shopping cart up. _____

5 It makes work easier. _____

Unit 2   17

4 What can these simple machines do? Read and circle.

1 A lever (can) / can't move things.
2 A pulley can / can't move an object sideways.
3 A wagon can / can't grasp objects like a ball.
4 A simple machine can / can't make work easier.
5 A wedge can / can't move a shopping cart.
6 You can / can't use an inclined plane to move a shopping cart.

> **Grammar Tip**
>
> Sometimes tools and machines **can** do things that your body **can't** do on its own.

5 Which simple machine can solve the problem? Read and write *an inclined plane* or *a pulley*.

1 **A:** I can't move the wood up to the treehouse.
   B: You can use _____*a pulley.*_____

2 **A:** I can't move the wheelchair into the house.
   B: You can use _____.

3 **A:** I can't move the apples down from the apple tree.
   B: You can use _____.

6 Classify the body parts and tools. Write them in the chart.

~~arms~~   tongs   knife   shovel   teeth   claws

Wedge	Levers
_____	*arms*
_____	_____
_____	_____

18 Unit 2

7 What simple machines do these animals have? Circle.

1 It can use its claws as **levers** / **(wedges)**.

2 It can use its flippers as **levers** / **wedges**.

3 It can use its beak as **wedges** / **levers**.

4 It can use its teeth as a **wedge** / **lever**.

8 What can they do? Match and write *levers* or *wedge(s)*.

1 A goat can eat grass.
2 A duck can swim.
3 A child can eat an apple.
4 A dog can dig.

a She can use her teeth as a _____.
b It can use its claws as _____.
c It can use its teeth as a __wedge.__
d It can use its feet as _____.

9 What can you do? Look and write.

1 I can __lift a bag.__ I can use my __arm__ as a __lever.__

2 I can _____. I can use my _____ as _____.

3 I can _____. I can use my _____ as _____.

4 _____

Unit 2   19

Unit 3
Plants and Animals

How do plants and animals live in their habitats?

1 Where do animals and plants live? Look, unscramble, and write.

1 __forest__ (trefos) 2 _____ (necoa)

3 _____ (serted) 4 _____ (dlandtew)

5 They are all _____ (tthbaias).

2 What do you know about the things in the photos? Look, read, and write.

coral   cactus   alligator   deer

1 It lives in wetlands. It eats meat. It's dangerous.   __alligator__

2 It lives in the forest. It eats plants.   _____

3 It's in the ocean. Fish live near it.   _____

4 It's in the desert. It doesn't need a lot of water.   _____

3 Read about habitats in Australia. Circle.

Come and visit "Down Under"! You will find four very different habitats.

New South Wales has more than 20,000 (**1**) wetlands / deserts. They provide habitats to a lot of animals. Be careful, though! Some of the animals, for example the (**2**) deer / alligators, are dangerous.

There are ten (**3**) deserts / forests in Australia. The Great Victoria is very hot, and there isn't a lot of rain, so there aren't many plants. But (**4**) cactuses / coral are able to grow there.

Australia has 2.5 million square kilometers of forests. In parts of Tasmania, New South Wales, and Victoria, you can see red, white, or black (**5**) alligators / deer in the forests.

The Pacific, Southern, and Indian are the three (**6**) wetlands / oceans around Australia. Many species of fish live there.

Reading Tip

Read the text quickly to look for the information you want. This is called scanning.

4 Look at 3. What do these numbers relate to? Write the words.

1 4: _habitats_   2 3: _____

3 20,000: _____   4 2,500,000 km²: _____

5 Imagine you live in Australia. What can you see in the different habitats? Write.

1 When I am in the desert, I can see _cactuses._

2 When _____, I _____.

3 _____

4 _____

Unit 3   21

Lesson 1 · What are some parts of animals?

1 Which animal body parts can you see? Look and write.

| claw | spike | ~~horns~~ | beak |

1 __horns__   2 _____   3 _____   4 _____

2 How do animals use their body parts? Read and match.

1 camouflage
2 poison
3 spikes
4 beak
5 claws
6 horns

a A pelican uses it to catch fish.
b Some frogs have it in their skin and use it to stay safe.
c An arctic fox uses them to dig in the snow.
d A porcupine fish uses them to protect itself.
e A horned lizard uses them to stay safe.
f This helps some lizards to hide from other animals.

3 How do other animals stay safe? Read and circle *T* (true) or *F* (false).

1 An arctic fox has a beak.   T /(F)
2 A crab spider uses camouflage.   T / F
3 A coral snake uses its claws to stay safe.   T / F
4 A lionfish uses its spikes to stay safe.   T / F
5 A pill bug uses its horns to stay safe.   T / F

4 Read about the lionfish. Write *its* or *it's*.

The Lionfish

The warm oceans around the world are (**1**) _its_ habitat. (**2**) _____ about 30 cm long. (**3**) _____ a dangerous fish. It keeps itself safe with (**4**) _____ spikes. They have lots of poison in them. It eats fish. Some fish try to hide from the lionfish in the coral, but (**5**) _____ fast.

Grammar Tip

A robin puts **its** beak into the soil to catch earthworms. **It's** very fast!

5 What do you remember about lionfish? Read and correct the sentences.

1 Lionfish live in ~~cold~~ water.   _warm_

2 It isn't a dangerous fish.   _____

3 It uses its horns to protect itself.   _____

4 It doesn't use poison to stay safe.   _____

5 It's slow.   _____

6 Write about the porcupine fish.

The Porcupine Fish

Habitat: warm oceans, reefs   Length: 20 cm

Keep itself safe: has spikes, drinks a lot of water and its body gets big, spikes stick out, has poison in body

Camouflage: no

_____ are its habitat. It's _____.

It keeps itself safe with _____

_____

_____.

Unit 3 23

Lesson 2 • What are the parts of plants?

1 What do plants need to grow? Unscramble and write.
Plants need…

1. rteaw
2. rai
3. treintusn
4. lnushtgi
5. pcase

__water__   _____   _____   _____   _____

2 How do the parts of the sunflower help it to grow? Read and write.

nutrients   sunlight   seeds   stem   ~~roots~~   soil

Monday, May 16, 2016

We are learning about plants at school, and we are growing a sunflower. Here's what I know! Plants have (1) __roots__ that grow in the (2) _____. They give the plant water and (3) _____. The (4) _____ carries them to the leaves. Leaves take in (5) _____ and air. They make food for the plant. A sunflower has (6) _____. They can grow into new plants. This is a photo of our sunflower!

3 What do the parts of a sunflower do? Circle T (true) or F (false).

1. Leaves grow into the soil.   T / **F**
2. The stem carries water to the leaves.   T / F
3. The roots take in sunlight.   T / F
4. Seeds can make new plants.   T / F
5. The roots take in nutrients.   T / F

Reading Tip

Read the sentences and underline the key words. Look for the key words in the text to find out if the sentences are true or false.

4 What do you know about the trees in the photos? Look and complete.

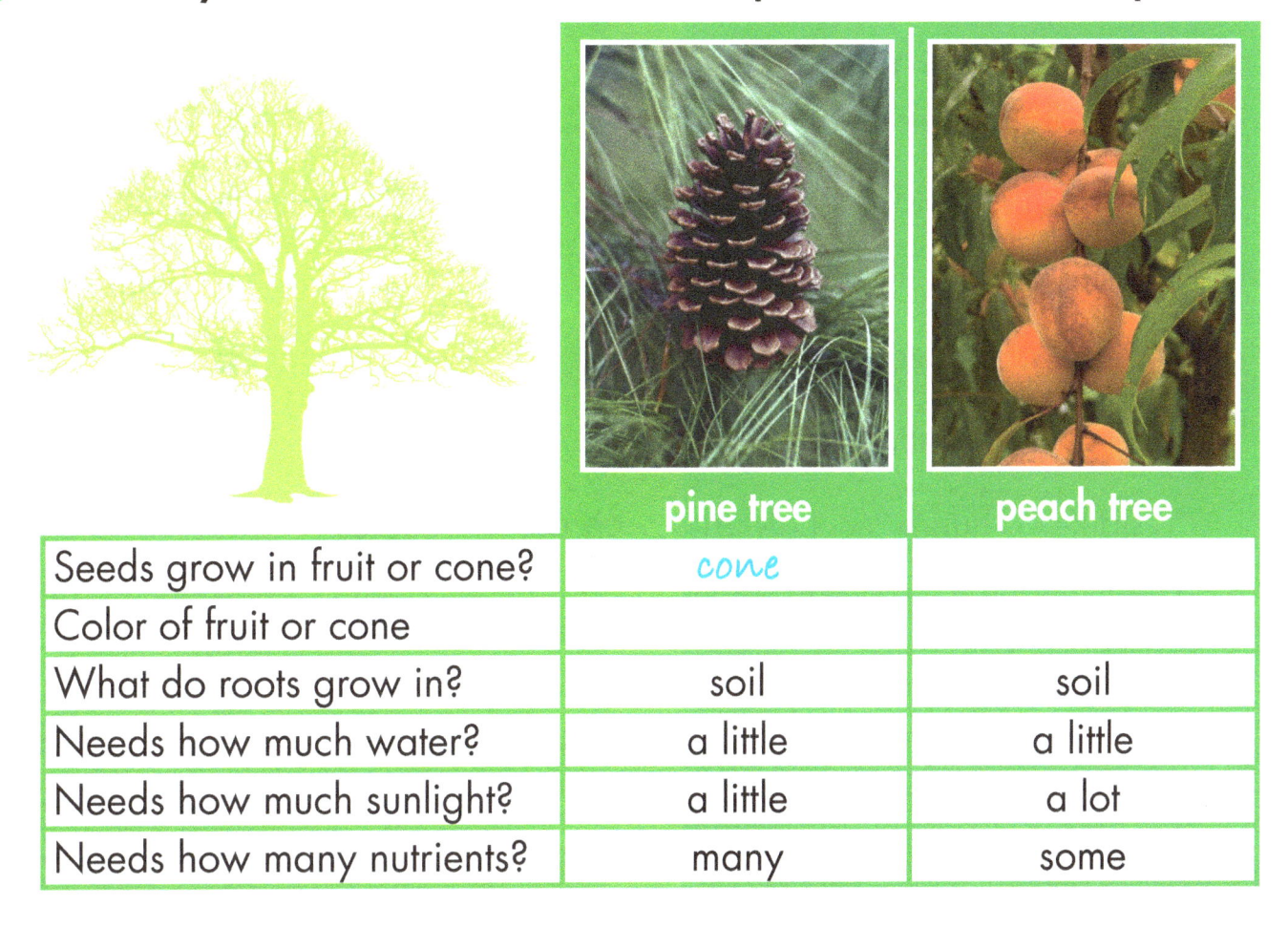

	pine tree	peach tree
Seeds grow in fruit or cone?	cone	
Color of fruit or cone		
What do roots grow in?	soil	soil
Needs how much water?	a little	a little
Needs how much sunlight?	a little	a lot
Needs how many nutrients?	many	some

5 Look at the chart in **4**. Write about the pine tree.

The pine tree grows from a (**1**) ___seed.___ The seeds grow inside (**2**) _____. They are (**3**) _____ in color. The (**4**) _____ of pine trees grow in (**5**) _____. It doesn't need a lot of water. Pine trees need a little (**6**) _____ to grow. They also need many different (**7**) _____ to grow.

6 Look at the chart in **4**. Write about the peach tree.

The peach tree grows from a seed. The seeds grow inside _____. They are _____ in color. The _____ of peach trees grow _____

_____.

Unit 3 25

Lesson 3 • Where do plants and animals live?

1 **Life in the desert. Read and match.**
1. A cactus holds water here.
2. A camel holds fat here.
3. This animal lives in the desert.
4. This plant lives in the desert.

a camel
b stalk
c cactus
d hump

2 **The desert habitat. Read and write.**

stalk   hump   ~~habitat~~   camel   cactus

My favorite (**1**) _habitat_ is the desert. It's very hot and there's little water. This makes it dangerous for people to live there. The people who live in the desert are called nomads. They look after goats, sheep, and camels.

My favorite animal is the (**2**) _____. It doesn't need a lot of water or food because it has a lot of fat in its (**3**) _____. This helps it live in dry places. I think it looks funny!

My favorite plant is the (**4**) _____. It doesn't need a lot of water. It can hold water in its (**5**) _____ and roots.

3 **What can you remember? Read and mark (✓) or (✗).**
1. The desert isn't very safe to live in. ✓
2. Nomads live in the desert.
3. A camel needs to eat.
4. A cactus doesn't need water.

26 Unit 3

4 Read about the arctic fox. Write *many, a lot of, little,* or *some.*

The arctic fox lives in the Arctic. It is a very cold habitat and can be -50 °C. There aren't (**1**) ___many___ trees where the arctic fox can find shelter. It makes a hole in (**2**) _____ snow, and it lives there.

The arctic fox has (**3**) _____ fur. It uses the fur as camouflage. In winter, its fur turns white to look like the snow. In summer, it's brown to look like the rocks and plants in its habitat.

The arctic fox eats small animals, birds, and fish. In winter, there's (**4**) _____ food. It follows large animals and eats the food that the large animals don't eat.

Grammar Tip

Many different plants and animals live in the ocean.
Plants that need **a lot of** water grow in a wetland.
Short plants get **little** or no sunlight.
Some plants and animals can live in the desert.

5 Read and write about the white-tailed deer.

White-tailed Deer
Habitat: North America
            Forests—Shelter
Looks: Uses camouflage
            Red/brown fur with white tail
Eats: Plants

The white-tailed deer lives in _____. There are a lot of _____. The deer uses _____. Its fur is _____ _____. It eats _____.

Unit 3   27

Review 1-3

1 Complete the crossword. Use the photos.

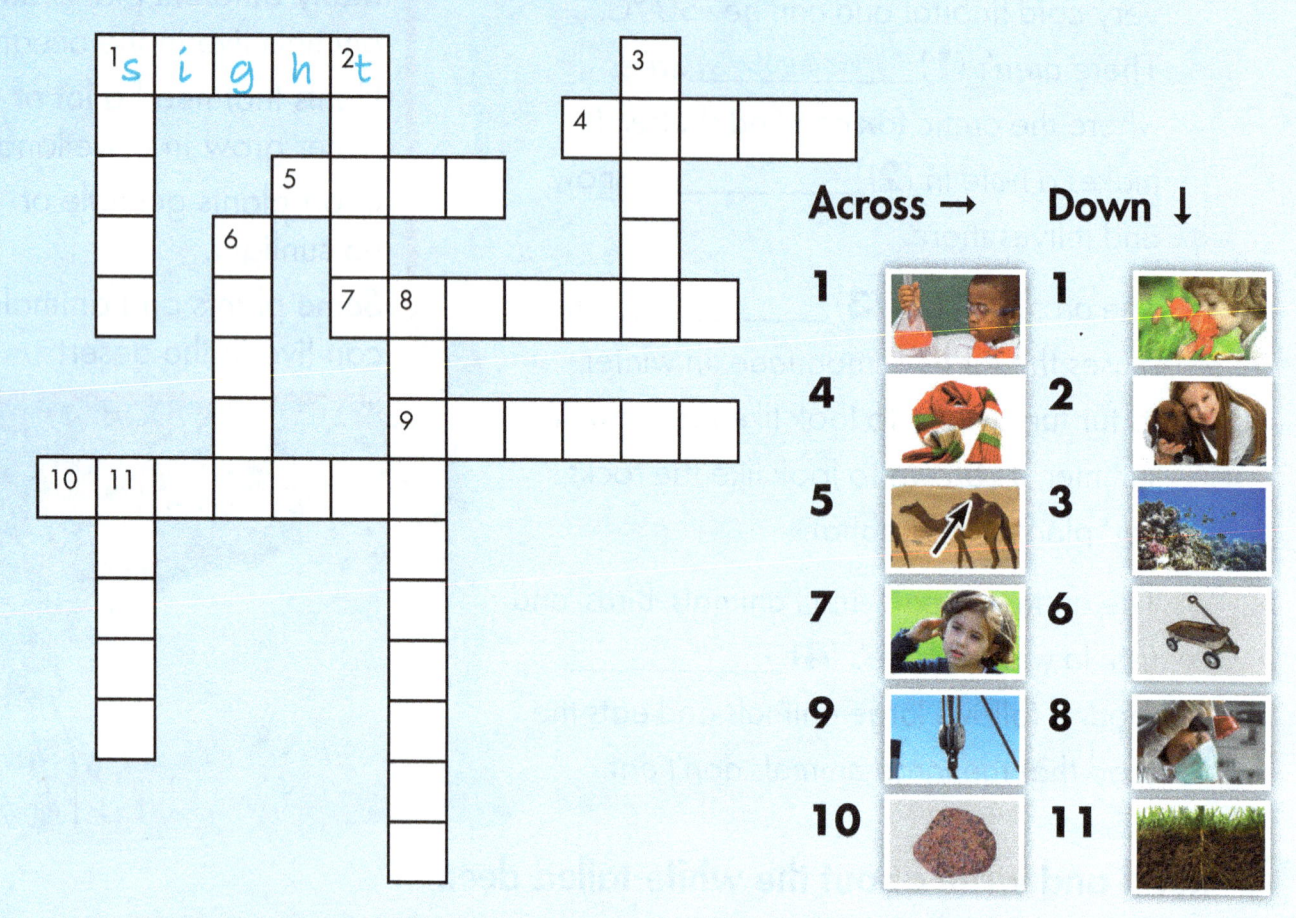

Across →
1, 4, 5, 7, 9, 10

Down ↓
1, 2, 3, 6, 8, 11

1 Across: s i g h t

2 Where do animals and plants live? Unscramble and write the words. What's the mystery word?

1 nceao — o c e a n

2 eesdtr

3 lnadewt

4 bihatta

Mystery word: f _ _ _ _ _

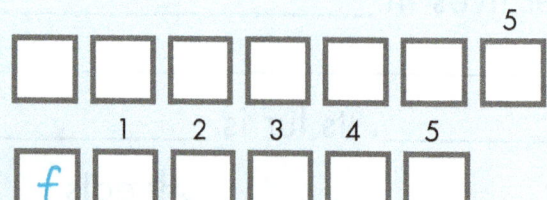

28 Review 1-3

3 What am I? Read, think, and write.

1 I am a heavy material.   c <u>o</u> <u>r</u> <u>d</u> <u>u</u> <u>r</u> <u>o</u> <u>y</u>

2 I move heavy objects up, down, and sideways.   p __ __ __ __ __

3 I am a rough rock.   p __ __ __ __ __

4 I am a simple machine. I make it easier to move things.   i __ __ __ __ __ __ __
                                                              p __ __ __ __

5 An animal uses me to dig.   c __ __ __ __

6 Plants grow in me.   s __ __ __

4 Look and write. Which is the odd one out?

1

<u>camouflage</u> _____ _____ _____

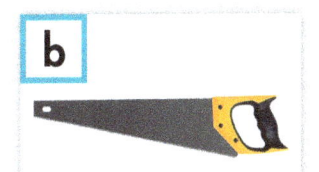

The odd one out is _____.

2

_____ _____ _____ _____

The odd one out is _____.

3

_____ _____ _____ _____

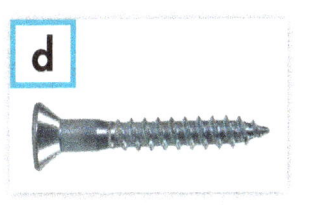

The odd one out is _____.

Review 1–3

Unit 4 Body and Growth

How do we grow and change?

1 What are the different stages of human development? Look, read, and write.

adolescent baby adult child

1 They are between ten and 17 years old.   _adolescent_
2 They go to school, and they have lots of energy.   _____
3 They are between one day old and two years old.   _____
4 They go to work every day.   _____

2 Read and write. Use the words from 1.

a (2 months old)   _baby_   b (8 years old)   _____
c (16 years old)   _____   d (30 years old)   _____

3 Look at 2. Read and write the letters. Then complete for you.

1 They brush their teeth.   [b] [c] [d]
2 They do their homework.   [ ] [ ]
3 They play with their toys.   [ ] [ ]
4 They can run and jump.   [ ] [ ] [ ]
5 I _____.

4 What do we need to be healthy? Read and write *baby, child, adolescent,* or *adult.*

Reading Tip

Look at the graphs, charts, and tables and underline the key words. They will help you find the answers.

Sleep is very important for everybody. It helps us grow and be healthy.

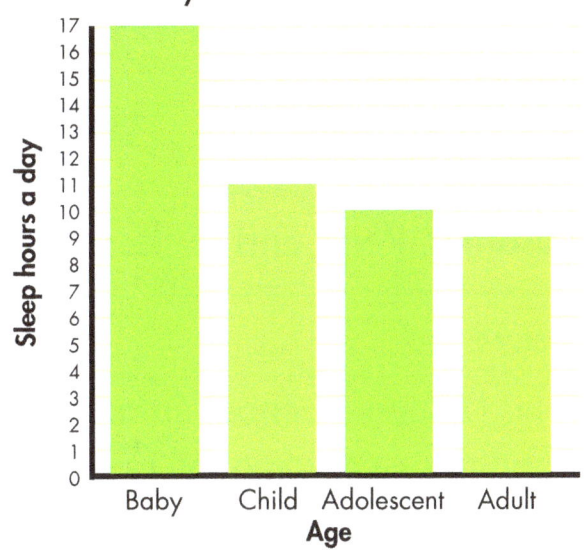

Food gives us energy to grow and develop. Its energy is measured in calories. Look at the calories we need:

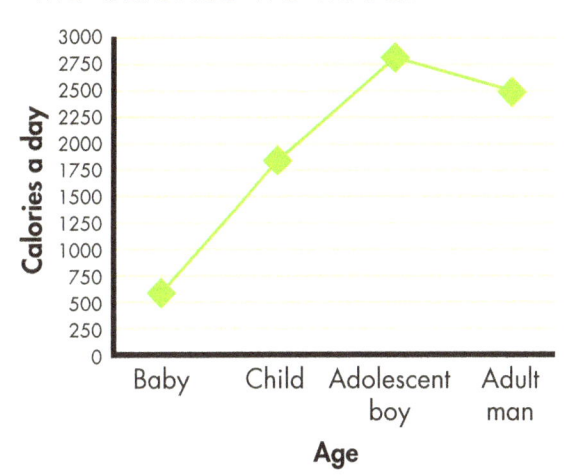

Exercise helps us have a healthy body, feel good, and sleep well.

Hours of Exercise a Week	
Child	7
Adolescent	7
30 years	3

1 He needs 600 calories a day.   _baby_

2 She needs to sleep for ten hours a day.   _____

3 She needs to sleep for nine hours a day.   _____

4 They need to exercise for one hour a day.   _____ _____

5 Look at the information in **4**. Complete for you.

I am a child. I need to sleep _____ a day. I need to eat _____. I need to exercise _____.

Lesson 1 • What are the stages of human development?

1 Human development. Look, match, and number in order.

infancy   adulthood   adolescence   childhood

a   b   c **1**   d

2 Sally is talking to Marie about her brother. Read and circle.

Marie:	Do you have a brother or sister?
Sally:	Yes, I have a brother. He's in his **(1)** adolescence / **(infancy)**. He's one year old. His **(2)** maturity / coordination isn't perfect. He often falls over.
Marie:	That's part of a baby's **(3)** physical / mental development.
Sally:	Do you have a brother or sister?
Marie:	Yes, I have one sister. She's sixteen and in her **(4)** childhood / adolescence.

3 How do we change throughout our lifetime? Read and write.

infancy   ~~maturity~~   childhood   mental

1 We reach this phase of life when we stop growing.   _maturity_

2 This is the phase of life before we are two years old.   _____

3 This is the phase of life between three and ten.   _____

4 These changes are related to our brains.   _____

32 Unit 4

4 What do you know about the development of babies? Read and write *our* or *their*.

Before they are one month old, babies sleep up to 17 hours a day.
(**1**) _____Their_____ sight isn't very good. At two months old, they can see well and (**2**) _____ hearing is good. At three months, babies know who we are. They know (**3**) _____ faces and (**4**) _____ voices when we talk to them. At six months, they can eat food and sit. At eight months, they can crawl and they start to stand up. At nine months, they can say (**5**) _____ first words. At twelve months, they can walk and help tidy up (**6**) _____ toys.

Grammar Tip

When human babies are born, they look a lot like **their** parents. But we change a lot throughout **our** lifetime.

5 Look at 4. Read and circle *T* (true) or *F* (false).

1 Babies sleep a lot in their first month.	**T** / F
2 They reach maturity at six months old.	T / F
3 They know who their parents are before they are one month old.	T / F
4 Their coordination is good at twelve months old.	T / F
5 Their senses are good at two months old.	T / F

Unit 4   33

6 Human activities. Read and mark (✓).

When do you usually…	Infancy	Childhood	Adolescence	Adulthood
1 reach maturity?				✓
2 color a picture?				
3 jump rope?				
4 do homework?				
5 cook a meal?				
6 have a baby?				
7 crawl?				

7 Look at 6. Write the activities in the correct place.

Infancy   Childhood   Adolescence   Adulthood

reach maturity

8 Look at 7. What activities do you do and don't you do? Write.

I am a child. I _____.

I don't _have a baby_____.

34 Unit 4

Lesson 2 • How do some parts of our bodies change as we grow?

1 **Our changing bodies. Circle, read, and write.**

tso(contracting)epskeletontunoxygeneadrelaxinglfjointmki

1 Muscles get shorter by doing this. _contracting_

2 This is in the air we breathe. We need it to live. _____

3 This is where two bones meet. _____

4 Muscles go back to their normal length when doing this. _____

5 This is all the bones in your body. _____

2 **How do our bodies work? Read and correct the sentences.**

1 Your ~~heart~~ sends messages to your body to tell it what to do. _brain_

2 Food goes into your heart. _____

3 Your brain carries oxygen to all parts of your body. _____

4 Joints move parts of the body by contracting and relaxing. _____

3 **How do muscles work? Read, look, and write the letters.**

☐ 1 When the muscles in my arm contract, they get shorter.

☐ 2 When they relax, they go back to their normal length.

a — Tendon, Biceps (relaxed), Origin, Humerus, Triceps (contracted), Ulna

b — Biceps (contracted), Triceps (relaxed), Radius, Insertion

Unit 4 35

4 Playing soccer. Read and write *First*, *Next*, or *Last*.

What happens to my body when I play soccer?

When I play soccer, I use my senses.
(1) __First__, I use my sight to see the ball.
(2) _____, my senses send information to my brain. (3) _____, my brain sends a message to my body to run.
When I run, I need oxygen. Oxygen is in the air. (4) _____, I breathe air. (5) _____, the heart pumps the blood to the lungs. (6) _____, the blood picks up oxygen in the lungs. (7) _____, the blood carries oxygen around the body.
When I run, the muscles in my legs are contracting and relaxing.

Grammar Tip

First, you see the ball. **Next**, you run toward it. **Last**, you catch it. **Then** can mean the same as **next**.

5 Look at 4. Read and answer the questions.

1 What sense does the boy use?　　　　　　__sight__

2 What sends his body the message to run?　_____

3 What is in the air that the body needs?　　_____

4 What moves blood to the lungs?　　　　　_____

5 What moves oxygen around the body?　　_____

6 What are his muscles doing when he runs?　_____

36　Unit 4

6 What do our bodies do when we play soccer? Order the information.

1 Brain
- ☐ a brain sends message to body to run
- ☐ 1 b use sight to see ball
- ☐ c senses send information to brain

2 Heart and lungs
- ☐ a heart pumps blood to lungs
- ☐ b breathe air
- ☐ c blood takes oxygen to body
- ☐ d blood picks up oxygen in lungs

7 What does our body do when we catch a ball? Order and write the information.

heart pumps blood to lungs
blood takes oxygen to body
blood picks up oxygen in lungs
brain tells us to catch
breathe air
senses send information to brain
~~use sight to see ball~~

Brain
1. use sight to see ball
2. _____
3. _____

Heart and Lungs
4. _____
5. _____
6. _____
7. _____

8 Write how to catch a ball. Look at 7.

First, I use my sense of sight to see the ball. Next, my senses _____
_____
_____
_____.

Unit 4 37

Unit 5 Earth's Materials

What is Earth made of?

1 Earth's different places. Look and write.

1. <u>o</u> c <u>e</u> <u>a</u> n
2. __ i __ __ __
3. l __ __ e
4. __ __ __ __ t __ i n s
5. r __ __ e __
6. g __ __ __ i __ r

2 Look at 1. Read and write.

a It's a large body of moving ice.   <u>glacier</u>

b It's a large area of water with land all around.   _____

c They are very big, and people climb them. There's often snow on top.   _____

d They are smaller than mountains.   _____

e It takes water into the ocean or lakes.   _____

f It covers most of the Earth.   _____

38   Unit 5

3 Look at the picture and title of the article in **4**. What is the article about?

_____

> **Reading Tip**
> Look at the picture and title before you start to read a text. This will help you understand the gist of the text.

4 Read and circle.

An Interesting Country

Iceland is in the North Atlantic (**1**) *Ocean* / *Lake*, south of the Arctic Circle. The (**2**) *environment* / *mountain* is very important to the people who live there.

(**3**) *Hills* / *Glaciers* cover about 11.5% of the country. They are made of ice. Hvannadalshnúkur is the highest (**4**) *mountain* / *river* in Iceland. It is 6,926 feet high. Many people like to climb it. There are also (**5**) *hills* / *lakes*, where Icelandic horses live. People can ride these horses or use them for farm work.

Water is important in Iceland. People can use the fast movement of water in (**6**) *rivers* / *glaciers* to get hot water for their homes. They can also get fish from the country's (**7**) *oceans* / *lakes*. There are about 60 of them in Iceland.

5 Describe your country. Think and write.

_____ is in _____. There are _____

_____. There is / are also _____

_____. People can _____

_____.

Unit 5   39

Lesson 1 • What are some kinds of land and water?

1 Land and water. Look and match the word halves.

| ream | ~~ndform~~ | nd | zen | esh | in | and | lty |

1. la_ndform_
2. po_____
3. st_____
4. pla_____
5. isl_____
6. fro_____
7. sa_____ water
8. fr_____ water

2 Classify the words.

| ~~mountain~~ | river | plain | island | ocean |
| hill | pond | lake | stream |

Landforms	Water
mountain	_____
_____	_____
_____	_____
_____	_____

40   Unit 5

3 Land and water on vacation. Read and write.

fresh   ~~island~~   ponds   landform   stream   plains

Tuesday, December 20, 2016

Hi Sally,

I am on vacation on the Isle of Wight. It's an (1) __island__ near the south of England. It's great! The surface of the island isn't flat. There aren't any (2) _____. The most common (3) _____ is hills.

Jasper, our dog, loves walking in the hills. He likes it when we get to a (4) _____ because he can drink the (5) _____ water. He also likes swimming in (6) _____. Mom isn't happy because he gets wet and dirty! At the beach, we throw Jasper a ball, and he catches it.

Today, we are at a lake where the water is frozen. It's my favorite place because we are ice-skating!

See you soon.

Love,

Claudia x

Reading Tip

The person or animal won't always be referred to by name. Pay special attention to pronouns.

4 Read and mark (✓).

Who...	Claudia	Mom	Jasper
1 is on vacation?	✓	✓	✓
2 loves walking in the hills?			
3 gets angry?			
4 swims?			
5 plays with the dog?			
6 likes ice-skating?			

5 What activities can you do in each environment? Read and write.

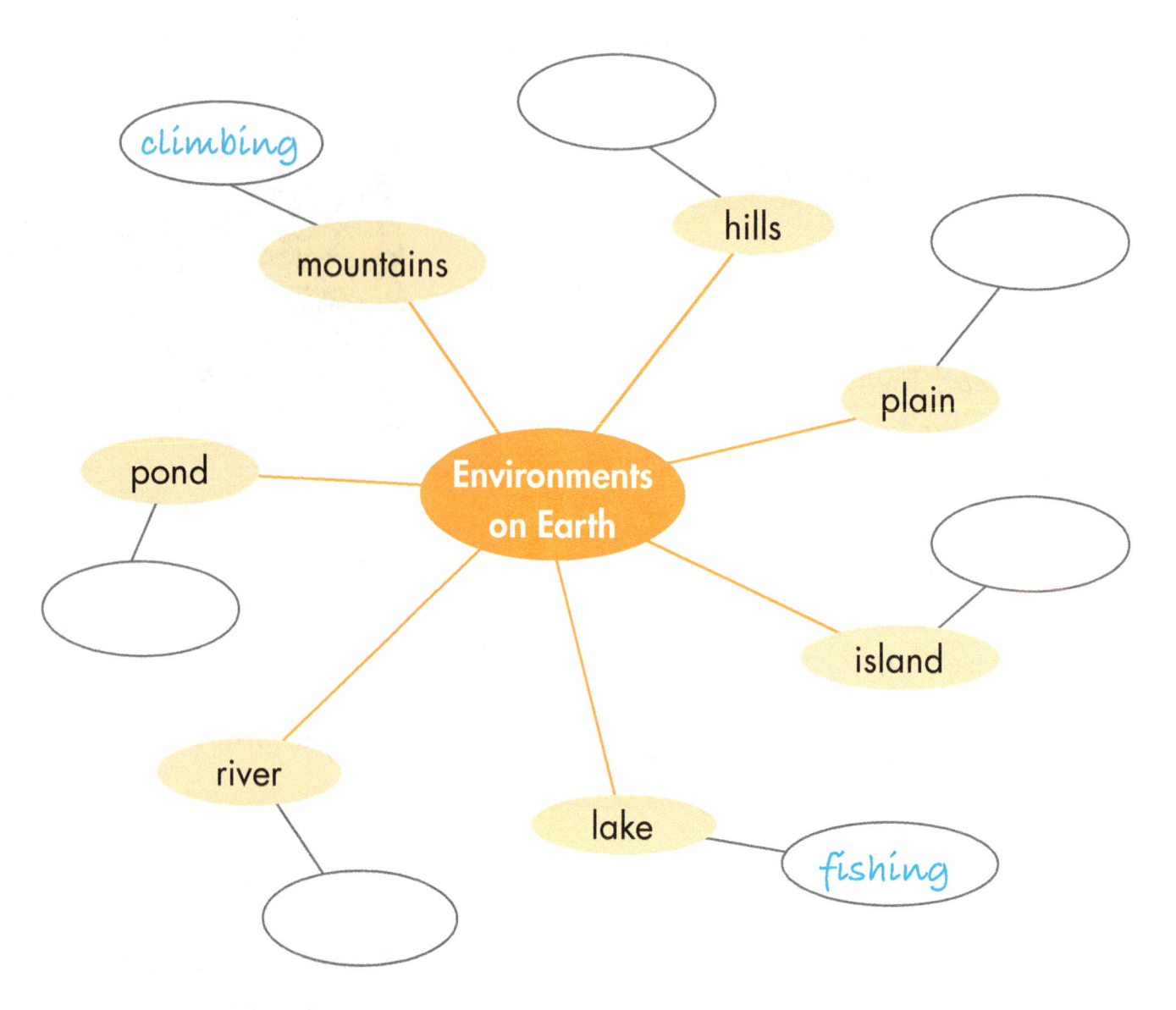

- mountains — climbing
- hills —
- plain —
- island —
- lake — fishing
- river —
- pond —

Environments on Earth

6 Imagine you are on vacation. What different environments are there? What are you doing there? Complete for you.

I am on vacation in _____. It's a _____.
There are _____
_____
_____
_____
_____.

Lesson 2 · How can people help protect Earth?

1 Helping the environment. Look, unscramble, and write.

ollpunoti   ccylree   ueers   frguee   edrcue

1. recycle
2. _____
3. _____
4. _____
5. _____

2 How can we help the environment? Read and write. Use the words from 1.

1 I can put plastic in the recycling bin.   recycle
2 I can pick up trash to help stop this.   _____
3 I can turn off the faucet to save water.   _____
4 I can write on both sides of the paper.   _____
5 I can give animals a safe place to live.   _____

Unit 5   43

3 Look at the photo and the title. What is the article about?

_____

Woodstock Animal Refuge: Saving Animals and Earth

Woodstock Animal Refuge gives 120 dogs a safe place to live. It provides young and old dogs with shelter and food. It also looks for families for the dogs to live with. John Smith, who works at the refuge, explains how they feel about the environment.

"We work to save animals, but we also want to save the environment. There are many things we do to save the environment. We ask people to give us their old dog beds and coats. We can use them again. We feed the dogs two times a day. That's 240 meals a day. We turn off the water when we do the dishes. We save a lot of water. When we feed the dogs, we recycle the metal cans. We ask the people who work here to put their paper, glass, and plastic in the recycling bins. We also ask them to pick up their trash. At the end of the day, we turn off all the lights. This saves money, too."

We can all help save the environment. It's easy!

4 Read and circle *T* (true) or *F* (false).

1 The refuge only gives young dogs a place to live.   T / **F**
2 It works to help the environment.   T / F
3 It doesn't buy new dog beds.   T / F
4 It feeds 240 dogs a day.   T / F
5 The people who work there recycle a lot of things.   T / F

5 Look at **3**. Underline all the ways this animal refuge protects Earth.

6 **What can you do to protect Earth? Write sentences using *can*. Think and write two more sentences.**

1 (pick up trash) <u>I can pick up trash.</u>
2 (walk to school) _____
3 (reuse paper) _____
4 (turn off water) _____
5 _____
6 _____

Grammar Tip

People **can** protect Earth by reducing the number of things they use.

I **can** reuse paper by writing on both sides.

7 **A notice for the refuge workers. Think and write. Use the ideas in 5.**

Are you helping to protect Earth?

Stop pollution: <u>You can pick up your trash.</u>
Reduce: _____
_____
Reuse: _____
Recycle: _____

8 **How can you help protect Earth? Write a notice for your class.**

Are you helping to protect Earth?

Stop pollution: _____
Reduce: _____
Reuse: _____
Recycle: _____

Unit 5   45

Unit 6 The Solar System

What are the sun, moon, and planets like?

1 What can you see in the photos? Look, unscramble, and match.

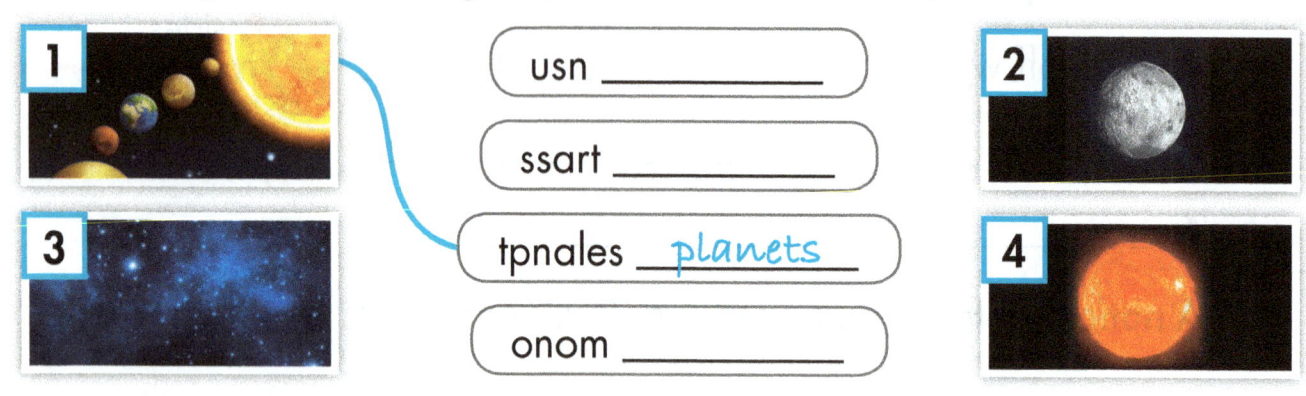

usn _____

ssart _____

tpnales __planets__

onom _____

2 The sky. Read and circle.

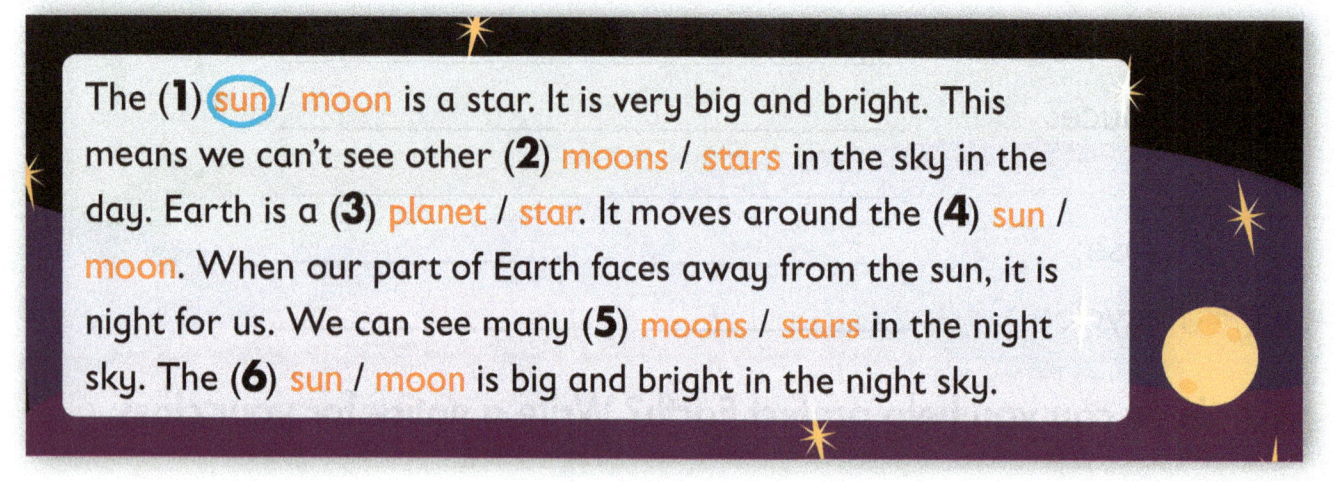

The (1) **sun** / moon is a star. It is very big and bright. This means we can't see other (2) moons / **stars** in the sky in the day. Earth is a (3) **planet** / star. It moves around the (4) **sun** / moon. When our part of Earth faces away from the sun, it is night for us. We can see many (5) moons / **stars** in the night sky. The (6) sun / **moon** is big and bright in the night sky.

3 Match the descriptions and the words from 1. Write.

1 They move around the sun. Earth is one of them.   __planets__

2 There are lots of these in the night sky.   _____

3 It is bright in the sky in the day.   _____

4 It looks big in the night sky.   _____

4 Look at the photo in **5**. What do you think the text is about? _____
_____

Reading Tip

What type of text is it? Is the language formal or informal? Think about the type of language you might find.

5 Read and write.

> moon   sun   stars   moon
> ~~planet~~   star   sun

February 15, 2016

Hello! My name is Sam. I am nine years old, and I live in Manchester, England. My **(1)** _planet_ is called Earth. <u>Which planet do you live on?</u>

I have a small family. There's my mom, my dad, and my brother, Jack. <u>Do you have a family?</u>

There's night and day on Earth. Earth moves around the **(2)** _____. It's a bright **(3)** _____. In the day, I go to school. At night, I watch television, and then I go to bed. From my bedroom window, I can see a lot of **(4)** _____ in the night sky. I can also see the **(5)** _____. <u>Can you see the **(6)** _____ in the day and the **(7)** _____ at night from your planet? What do you do in the day and night?</u>

6 Imagine you live on another planet. Write a reply to Sam. Answer his underlined questions in **5**.

Hi Sam,
My name is _____. I live on _____. _____
_____
_____
_____

Unit 6   47

Lesson 1 • What is the sun?

1 What do the pictures show? Look, circle, and write.

thy (light) furnt sunset byq heat byf noon sunrise

1. light
2. _____
3. _____
4. _____
5. _____

2 The sun. Read and write. Use the words from **1**.

What is the sun?

The sun is a star. It is a big ball of hot, glowing gases. We can't see other stars in the sky when the sun is shining because it is very bright.

Why is it important?

It's important because it gives Earth energy. We get (1) __light__ from the sun, and this energy gives us (2) _____. Most living things need light and heat. We need heat to keep warm. Fruit and vegetables need light and heat to grow.

Does it move?

The sun looks low in the morning at (3) _____, high at (4) _____, and low in the evening at (5) _____. It looks like the sun moves across the sky during the day. But the sun doesn't move. Earth moves around the sun.

48   Unit 6

3 John's vacation blog. Read and circle.

For a week every summer, we stay in a house by the beach. At (**1**) *sunrise* / *sunset*, when the day starts, my dad runs on the beach, but I usually sleep until 10 A.M.! Mom cooks lunch at 12 P.M. every day. In the afternoon, we go to the beach. We don't go there at (**2**) *sunset* / *noon* because the (**3**) *sun* / *moon* is high in the sky and it's very hot. The (**4**) *heat* / *bright* from the sun is very strong. We arrive at the beach at 3 P.M. and we leave at (**5**) *sunset* / *sunrise*, about 7.00 P.M.

Grammar Tip

The sun looks low in the sky in the morning **at sunrise**.
It looks high in the sky **at noon**.
It looks low in the sky in the evening **at sunset**.

4 Look at 3. When do they do these things? Write.

1 (John's dad / run)
John's dad runs at sunrise.

2 (John / sleep)
_____

3 (John's mom / cook lunch)
_____

4 (John's family / go home)
_____

5 When do you do different things on the weekend? Write.

On Saturday, I _____ at sunrise. I _____.
At _____ I _____. At _____
_____
_____.

Unit 6 49

Lesson 2 · What are the moon and stars?

1 What can you see in the photos? Read and circle.

1	2	3	4	5
stars / (craters)	moon / constellation	craters / stars	phases / constellation	stars / phases of the moon

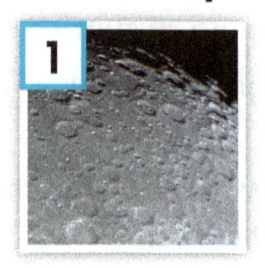

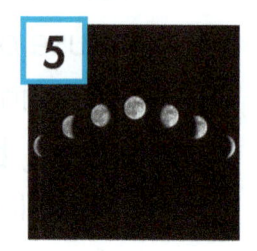

2 The moon. Read and write. Use the words from 1.

There are a lot of (1) __stars__ in the night sky. Some make pictures called (2) _____. But there is only one (3) _____. It looks bright in the sky because it reflects light from the sun. When the part of the moon reflecting the sun's light is facing Earth, we say there is a full moon. When the part of the moon reflecting the sun's light is not facing Earth, you can't see the moon. We say there is a new moon. The shape of the lighted part of the moon is called a (4) _____. The moon is made of rock. It has mountains and big (5) _____. These form when a big rock from space hits the moon.

3 Classify the words.

full new sunrise	
~~constellation~~ noon	
heat half crater	
light phase sunset	

Moon and Stars	Sun
constellation	_____
_____	_____
_____	_____
_____	_____
_____	_____
_____	

50 Unit 6

4 The night sky. Read and write *look, looks, look like,* or *looks like.*

Grammar Tip

The sun **looks** low in the morning at sunrise. This constellation **looks like** a lion.

Stars are big balls of burning gases that produce heat and light. From Earth, they **(1)** __look__ the same, but they are different colors and sizes. They **(2)** _____ small because they are far away. The moon **(3)** _____ big in the sky because it is close to Earth. Constellations are groups of stars that **(4)** _____ pictures in the sky. They usually **(5)** _____ animals or people. This is Orion. It's a constellation of many stars. It **(6)** _____ a hunter.

5 Two different constellations of stars. Look and write.

This is Leo. It's a __constellation.__
It looks _____.

This is Cancer. _____.
_____.

6 Draw your own constellation and write about it.

This is _____.
It's _____
_____
_____.

Unit 6 51

Lesson 3 • What is the solar system?

1 What are the names of the planets in the solar system? Look and write.

a The <u>s o l a r   s y s t e m</u>
b V __ __ __ s
c __ __ r __ h
d M __ __ __
e U __ __ __ u __
f __ e __ __ __ r __
g __ __ __ i __ e r
h __ a t __ r __
i __ __ __ t __ n __

2 What is the correct order of the planets? Write the words from 1.

1 <u>Mercury</u>   2 _____   3 _____   4 _____
5 _____   6 _____   7 _____   8 _____

3 Our solar system. Read and circle.

There are eight (1) (planets)/ constellations and their moons in our (2) solar system / path. They move around the (3) moon / sun, which is in the center. This path around an (4) object / orbit is called an (5) object / orbit. Most planets are different colors. The orbit of each planet is different because of its distance from the (6) solar system / sun. When the planet is close to the sun, it orbits the sun fast. When the planet is far away from the sun, it orbits the sun slowly. Earth's orbit takes 365 days. Neptune's orbit takes 165 years!

4 The inner planets. Read and complete the table.

The four inner planets are called Mercury, Venus, Earth, and Mars. They are all made of rock and metal. They all have mountains and craters. Mercury is next to the sun. Its orbit takes 88 days. It doesn't have a moon, and it's very hot. It can be 427 °C. Venus is next to Mercury. It's a very bright planet. On a clear day, you can sometimes see it in the sky. It doesn't have a moon, and it's very hot. It is 462 °C. It takes 225 days to move around the sun. Next, there's Earth. Its orbit takes 365 days. This is one year. It has one moon, and it can be 58 °C. Then there is Mars. It has two moons, Phobos and Deimos. It's very cold. It is 5 °C. Its orbit takes 686 days.

Reading Tip

Look at the table and think about what information you need to find. For example, is it a number or a specific word? Read and underline them in the text.

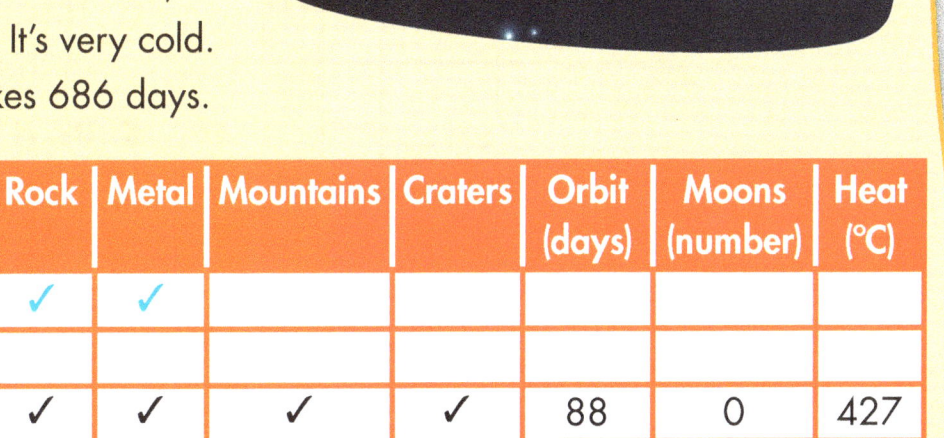

	Planet Number	Rock	Metal	Mountains	Craters	Orbit (days)	Moons (number)	Heat (°C)
Venus	2	✓	✓					
Mars								
Mercury	1	✓	✓	✓	✓	88	0	427
Earth								

5 Look at 4. Choose one of the planets and write about it.

The planet is called _____. It's made of _____.
It has _____. Its orbit _____
_____.

Review 4-6

1 **Complete the crossword. Use the clues.**

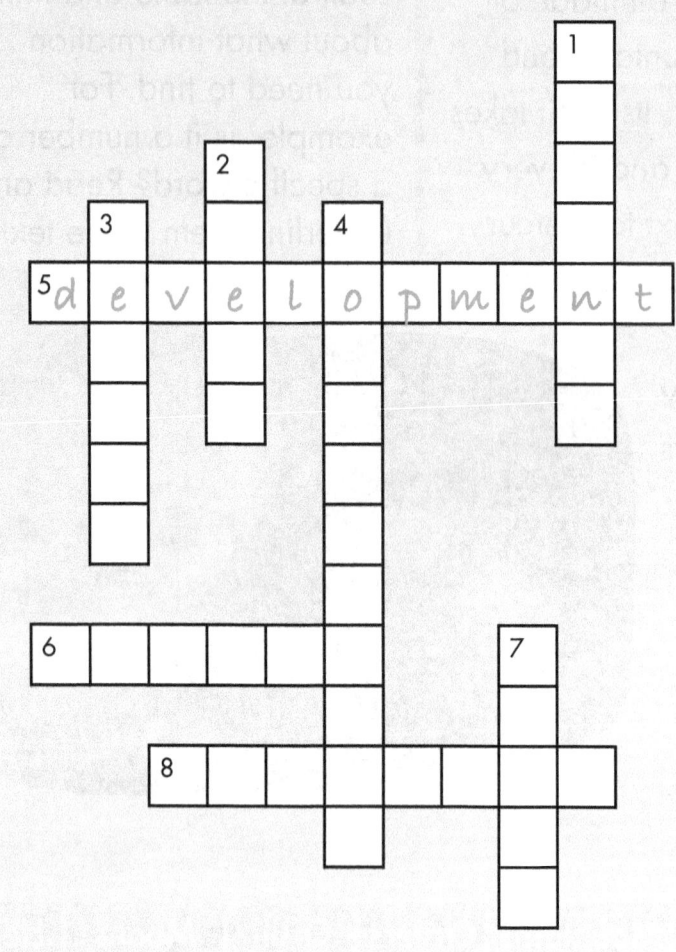

5 across: d e v e l o p m e n t

Down ↓

1 This is the stage of our lives when we are babies.
2 Coral and fish live in it.
3 This place looks after animals.
4 Some of my muscles are doing this when I bend my arm.
7 This is where two bones meet.

Across →

5 The process of growing and changing in our lives.
6 This is when the sun looks low in the sky in the evening.
8 It's a big landform. It often has snow at the top.

2 **Correct the sentences.**

1 ~~Their~~ coordination isn't perfect when we are babies. _____Our_____

2 The sun is a planet. _____

3 At noon, I get up and go running before the weather gets hot. _____

4 This constellation looks a lion. _____

5 First, we are children. Last, we are adolescents. _____

54   Review 4-6

3 Look at the photos and find the words in the wordsearch.

a	l	t	r	e	u	g	w	i	u	s
g	t	c	k	v	x	l	h	o	m	k
t	v	h	z	f	s	a	a	l	g	e
m	b	i	p	n	s	c	g	k	n	l
p	o	l	l	u	t	i	o	n	e	e
s	p	d	y	c	r	e	c	f	v	t
b	p	h	j	p	y	r	g	e	i	o
k	d	o	j	r	i	v	e	r	j	n
q	t	o	n	r	e	c	y	c	l	e
a	m	d	z	d	x	d	w	h	b	o

4 How much do you know about the solar system? Do the quiz.

1 How many planets are there in the solar system?
   a five   **b** eight   **c** twelve

2 What is the sun?
   a a moon   **b** a planet   **c** a star

3 Which planet is next to the sun?
   a Earth   **b** Saturn   **c** Mercury

4 What is a constellation?
   a a group of stars   **b** a group of planets   **c** a group of moons

5 What is the phase of the moon when you can see a small part of it?
   a a full moon   **b** a half moon   **c** a new moon

Review 4–6 55

Unit 7 Weather

How does weather change over time?

1 What can you see in the photos? Look and match with the headings in **2**.

1. a
2.
3.

2 Different kinds of weather. Classify the words.

~~snowy~~   cool
hot   rainy
dry   warm
cold   sunny

a Precipitation	b Temperature	c Drought
snowy		

3 Descriptions of weather. Read and correct the sentences.

1 A ~~thunderstorm~~ happens when it's very dry.   drought

2 When there's a rainbow, plants can't grow.   _____

3 Temperature happens when water falls from clouds.   _____

4 Words to describe rainbows are *hot* and *cold*.   _____

5 We can see a lot of colors in the sky when there's a drought.   _____

56 Unit 7

4 Changes in the weather. Read and write.

precipitation   ~~Weather~~   thunderstorm
Drought   temperature   rainbow

(1) _Weather_ in Hong Kong

April 17, 2016 13:07
The (2) _____ is 21 °C. There is a heavy (3) _____. It is very windy and rainy.

April 17, 2016 14:00
It is 25 °C and mainly sunny. There is a little (4) _____. Look out for a (5) _____!

⚠️ **WEATHER WARNING**
(6) _____ in Sichuan province. No rain for six weeks!

Reading Tip

Look at the headings in the fact file to understand what information you need. Be careful! The text doesn't always use the same words.

5 What is a rainbow? Read and write.

Did you know?

A rainbow is not an object. It is light. Water from the rain in the sky reflects sunlight, and this is the rainbow we see. There are six colors in a rainbow.

Rainbows

Weather: We can see rainbows when there is (1) _precipitation_ and it is (2) _____ at the same time.

A rainbow is: (3) _____. It isn't (4) _____.

What happens: Water in the sky reflects (5) _____.

Colors: (6) _____

Unit 7   57

Lesson 1 • How can you describe the weather?

1 Which words are connected to precipitation? Mark (✓).

windy	☐	humid	☐
snowy	✓	drought	☐
stormy	☐	sunny	☐
foggy	☐	sleet	☐
rainy	☐	wet	☐
hail	☐	icy	☐
dry	☐	freezing	☐

2 Read and write. Use words from **1**.

1 Where are you? I can't see anything. It's __foggy__.

2 It's a mixture of rain and snow. It's _____.

3 Balls of frozen rain are falling from the sky. It's _____.

4 The temperature is –5 °C. It's _____.

5 I'm in the jungle and it's wet and hot. It's _____.

6 There's a lot of rain and the wind is very strong. It's _____.

> **Grammar Tip**
>
> Hail is balls of frozen rain that fall **forcefully** from the clouds. Sleet falls more **softly** than hail.

3 How is the weather today? Complete for you.

It's _____.

58   Unit 7

4 How is the weather? Read and write the adverb.

1 The hail is falling _forcefully_ (forceful).

2 The sleet is falling _____ (soft).

3 The rain is falling _____ (loud).

4 The snow is falling _____ (quiet).

5 A weather map for the UK. Look, read, and circle.

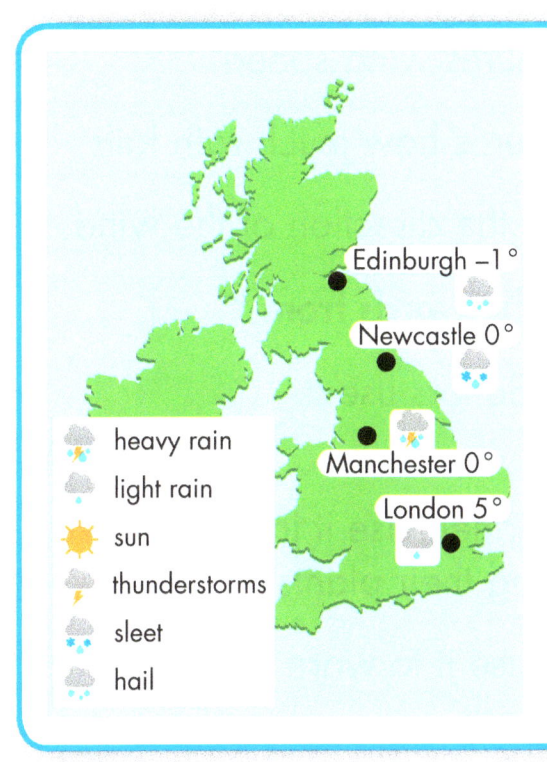

Today, there is a lot of (1) (precipitation) / drought. It's (2) dry / wet nearly everywhere! In Manchester, rain is falling (3) softly / forcefully. There are also thunderstorms. You may see some (4) snowy / sleet in Newcastle. In London, rain is falling (5) forcefully / softly. In Edinburgh, there's (6) icy / hail. The (7) temperature / precipitation is low everywhere, and it's (8) humid / freezing in the north.

6 A different weather map for the UK. Look and write.

Today, there's a mixture of weather. In London, it's (1) _sunny_, but in Manchester, (2) _____. In Newcastle, (3) _____. Scotland has very bad weather. In Edinburgh, (4) _____, and in Aberdeen, (5) _____.

Unit 7 59

Lesson 2 • How can you measure weather?

1 What do these objects measure? Look, circle, and match.

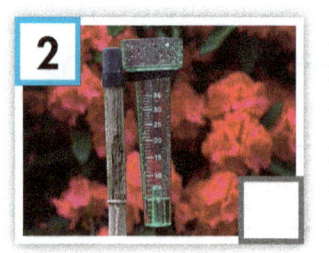

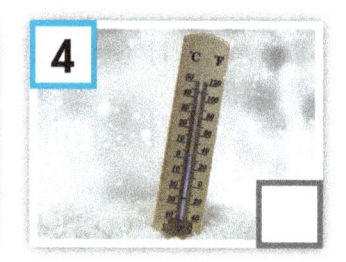

1	2	3	4
b			

a A **thermometer** / **anemometer** measures temperature.

b An **wind vane** / (**anemometer**) measures wind speed.

c A **rain gauge** / **thermometer** measures how much rain falls.

d A **anemometer** / **wind vane** shows the direction of the wind.

2 What are they? Read and write. Use the words from 1.

1 It shows the direction of the wind. Sailors use it when they sail their boat. _____wind vane_____

2 It measures how much rain falls. Farmers use it in their fields. It's important for growing their plants. _____

3 It measures wind speed. Scientists use it to warn people about storms with strong winds. _____

4 It measures temperature. Doctors use it to measure the temperature of a person who is sick. _____

3 Which weather tool? Read and match.

1 Is it hot today?   a Use an anemometer.
2 Did it rain a lot last night?   b Use a wind vane.
3 How windy is it today?   c Use a rain gauge.
4 Where is the wind coming from? d Use a thermometer.

60 Unit 7

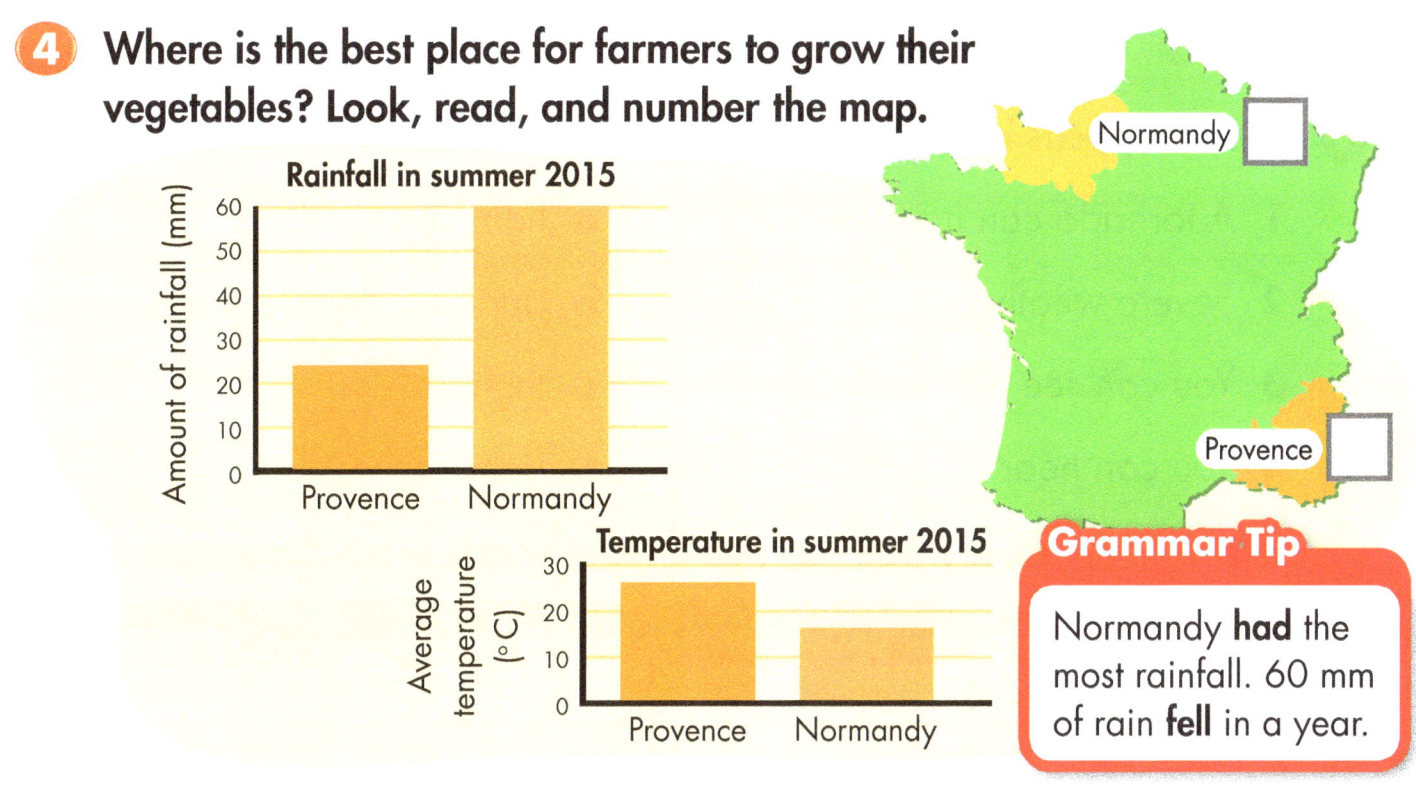

4 Where is the best place for farmers to grow their vegetables? Look, read, and number the map.

Normandy ☐

Provence ☐

Grammar Tip

Normandy **had** the most rainfall. 60 mm of rain **fell** in a year.

1 Farmer 1 wants to grow tomatoes. They like a little water, and a lot of sunlight and heat. The temperature needs to be hot but below 32 °C.

2 Farmer 2 wants to grow potatoes. They like a lot of water. They can grow in cold weather. The temperature needs to be below 26 °C.

5 Growing vegetables in Provence. Write verbs in the simple past.

Provence is a good place to grow tomatoes. Tomatoes like a lot of sunlight and heat. In 2015, Provence (**1**) ___was___ hot. Provence (**2**) _____ an average summer temperature of 27 °C. Tomatoes don't like a lot of rain. In Provence in summer 2015, a little rain (**3**) _____. The average rainfall (**4**) _____ 24 mm.

6 Growing potatoes in Normandy. Look at 4 and 5 and write.

Normandy is a good place to grow potatoes. Potatoes like _____
_____
_____
_____.

Unit 7 61

Lesson 3 • How can you stay safe in severe weather?

1 What happens in severe weather? Read and match.

1 A tornado can happen — a lightning.
2 Severe weather is — b during a thunderstorm.
3 You can see   c thunder.
4 You can hear   d dangerous.

2 Think and mark (✓). You can mark some words more than once.

	Thunderstorm	Hurricane	Tornado
Strong winds			
Heavy rain			
Thunder	✓		
Lightning			

3 Weird weather. Read and write.

~~thunder~~   severe weather   tornado
lightning   shelter   thunderstorm

May 3, 2016

Last night, we had terrible weather. Rain fell forcefully, and it was really windy. Next, I heard (1) _thunder_, and I saw (2) _____ in the sky. It was a (3) _____! Then, I looked out of the window, and I saw a (4) _____ coming toward the house. Luckily, I knew what to do. I moved away from the window, and I found (5) _____ under my bed! I was so scared.

Tell us your stories about strange or (6) _____!

62 Unit 7

4 Read and circle *T* (true) or *F* (false).

A Dangerous Job

Chevy Meyers looks for tornadoes in the United States. When I ask him why he does it, he says, "I live in Mississippi. In 2015, we had many tornadoes. They happen very quickly. I look for tornadoes because I want to learn how to predict them. People then have time to find shelter. I use a thermometer to measure the temperature, an anemometer to measure wind speed, and a wind vane to measure the direction of the wind. These tools help me in my job."

1 A tornado is thunder and lightning. T / **(F)**
2 Chevy Meyers runs away from tornadoes. T / F
3 Mississippi has a lot of tornadoes. T / F
4 Chevy doesn't use any tools. T / F

5 What do you do in a tornado? Read and write.

Sit   Cover   ~~Find~~   Stay

Grammar Tip
Go to the basement or an inside room.

1 __Find__ shelter in a building.   2 _____ near an inner wall.
3 _____ your head.   4 _____ away from windows.

6 What do you do in a thunderstorm? Read and write.

stay   turn off   close   the windows   in a building   the TV

1 _____
2 _____
3 _____

Unit 7 63

Unit 8 Matter

What is matter?

1 Different states of matter. Look, read, and mark (✓) or correct.

| 1 | 2 | 3 | 4 |

1 It's a ~~solid~~.   ___gas___　　　2 It's a gas. _____

3 It's a liquid. _____　　　4 It's a solid. _____

2 What kinds of matter are they? Read and circle.

1 A screw is a (solid) / gas.　　2 Oxygen is a gas / liquid.

3 Rain is a liquid / gas.　　4 Orange juice is a solid / liquid.

5 Oxygen isn't a gas / solid.　　6 A pen is a liquid / solid.

3 Read and draw lines.

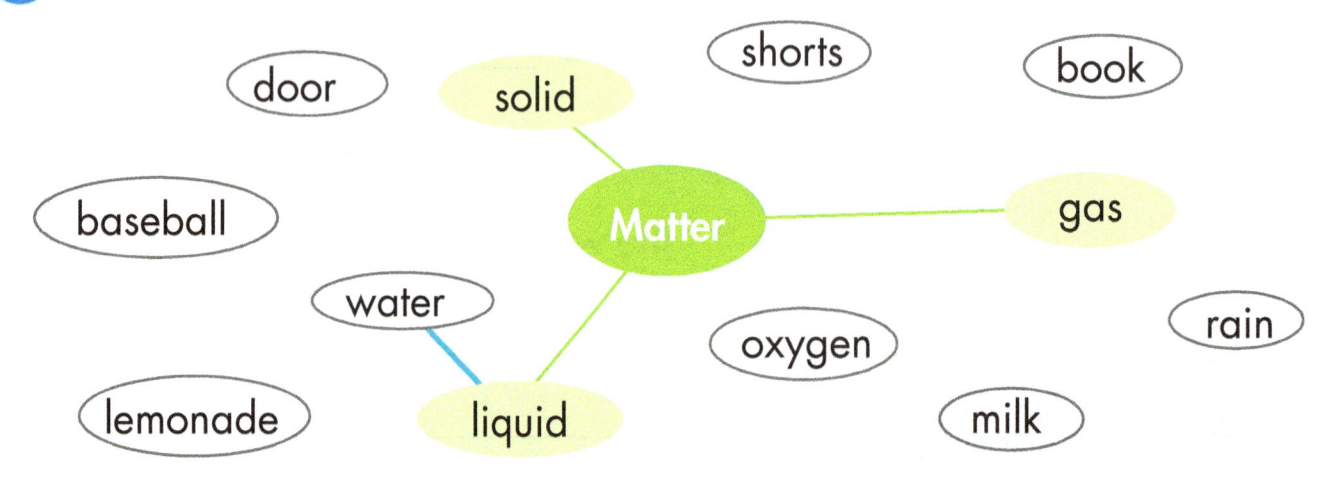

door, solid, shorts, book

baseball, Matter, gas

water, oxygen, rain

lemonade, liquid, milk

64 Unit 8

4 **Different states of matter in a garden. Read and write *solid*, *liquid*, or *gas*.**

Reading Tip

Look at the photo and think about which states of matter different items are made of. This will help you write the correct words in the text.

In my garden, there are some trees. A tree is a (**1**) __solid__. Next to them is a pond. The water in the pond is a (**2**) _____. I can see plants and flowers in the garden, too. A plant is a (**3**) _____. A flower is also a (**4**) _____. Are there any birds in the sky? A bird is a (**5**) _____. There is oxygen in the sky. Oxygen is a (**6**) _____.

5 **Different states of matter in a park near your home. Draw and write.**

In my park, there are some _____
_____
_____
_____.

Unit 8 **65**

Lesson 1 · What are solids, liquids, and gases?

1 What can you see in the photo? Look, circle, and write.

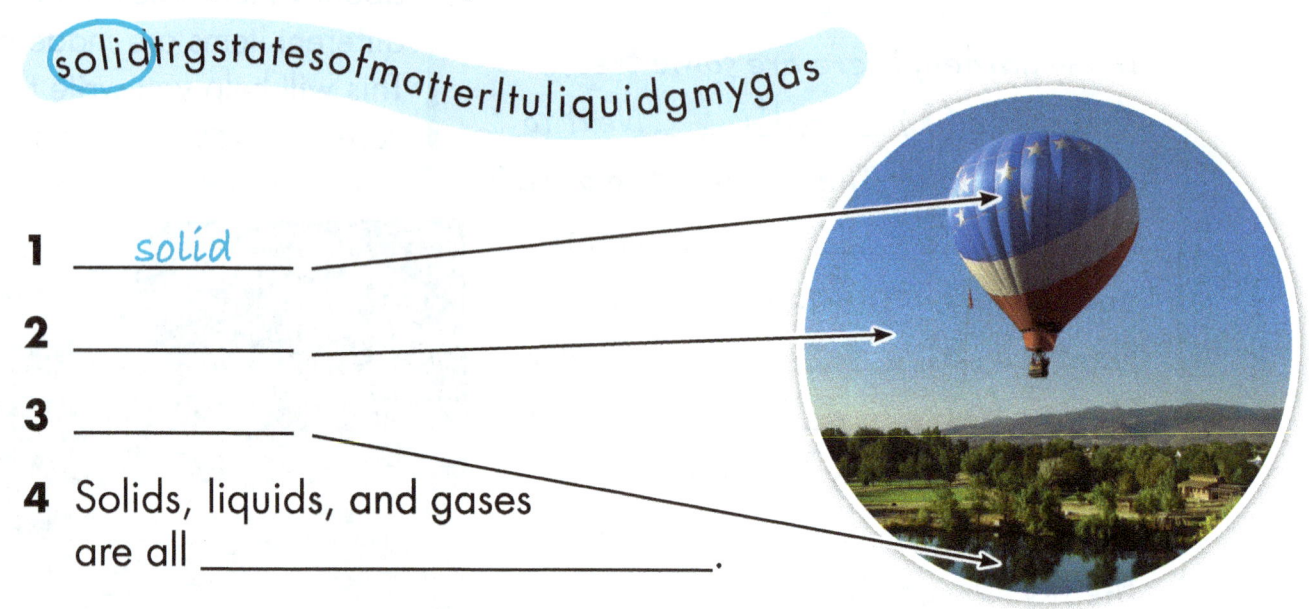

(solid)trgstatesofmatterltuliquidgmygas

1 _solid_

2 _____

3 _____

4 Solids, liquids, and gases are all _____.

2 Solid, liquid, or gas? Read the text and underline words for each. Then write. The photo in **1** can help you.

Fly in a hot air balloon!

See the beautiful hills, lakes, and rivers of Derbyshire and the Peak District.

We fly every day one hour after sunrise and two hours before sunset.

When there's a lot of rain, we cannot fly.

We fly for one hour. There's lots of time to take photos. So bring your camera!

We fly low so we don't carry oxygen.

Anyone can fly with us, but you need to be over 1.35 m tall to be able to see.

Call **0741 797265** for more information.

Solid

hot air balloon

_____

_____

Liquid

_____

_____

_____

Gas

_____

_____

3 Solids, liquids, and gases. Read and write *always* or *never*.

A solid (**1**) __always__ keeps its own size and shape. Solids (**2**) _____ take up space and have weight.

A liquid (**3**) _____ has its own shape. Liquids (**4**) _____ take the shape of their containers.

Gas (**5**) _____ has its own size or shape. Gas (**6**) _____ takes the size and shape of its container. It (**7**) _____ takes up all of the space inside the container.

> **Grammar Tip**
>
> It **always** keeps the same size and shape. Gas **never** has its own size and shape.

4 Size and shape. Look at 3 and complete the table with *always* or *never*.

	Keeps Its Own Shape	Keeps Its Own Size	Takes the Shape of Its Container, e.g. bowl, cup, etc.
Solid	always		
Liquid		always	
Gas			

5 The three states of matter. Think of examples. Write.

1 A _____ is a _____. It _____.

2 A _____ is a _____. It _____.

3 _____ is a _____. It _____.

Unit 8   67

Lesson 2 • What are some ways matter can change?

1 How can matter change? Look and match.

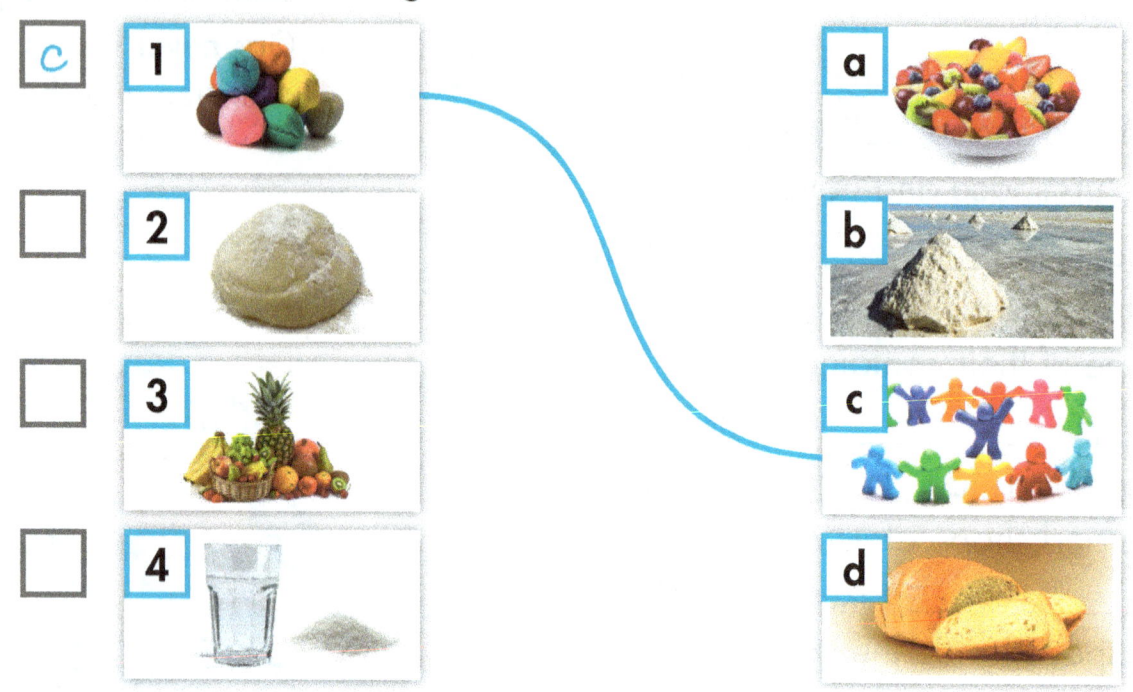

c 1
   2
   3
   4

a
b
c
d

2 Read and write.

> evaporate   physical change   ~~dough~~
>   mixture   clay   separate

A You can change __dough__ completely. You can put it in the oven to make bread.

B A fruit salad is a _____ of different fruits. You can _____ the fruit in the salad.

C You can mold this matter to make different shapes. The matter is called _____. Molding is an example of a _____.

D When there is a mixture of water and salt, the water can _____ in the sun. This changes the matter from a liquid to a gas.

3 Match the photos in **1** with the descriptions in **2**. Read and write A–D in **1**.

4 Can matter change? Read and write *can* or *can't*.

SCIENCE TODAY

Lizzie8: Can an object change? Can it become a new kind of matter?

Clever1: An object (**1**) __can't__ change and become a new object. You can cut paper. The size and shape changes, but it is still paper. You (**2**) _____ mold clay into a new shape. It is still clay.

Lizzie8: Thanks. ☺

Sam007: Can some things change completely?

Clever1: Yes! You (**3**) _____ change dough into bread when you put it in the oven. You (**4**) _____ change it back into dough.

Sam007: Thanks!

Peter123: My brother says you can't separate the parts in a mixture. Is this true?

Clever1: No, it isn't! For example, you (**5**) _____ separate the parts in a fruit salad.

Peter123: Can you separate the parts in a water mixture?

Clever1: Yes, you can. With water and salt, you (**6**) _____ evaporate the water. The water with the salt changes from a liquid to a gas.

Peter123: Thanks!

> **Grammar Tip**
> Matter **can** be changed.
> Baked bread **can't** be changed back into dough.

5 Look at 4 and write. Use *can* and the verb.

1 You __can cut__ paper. This is a physical change.

2 You _____ dough into bread. This is a complete change.

3 You _____ the parts in a fruit salad.

4 Water _____ in a water and salt mixture.

Unit 8   69

Lesson 3 • How can water change?

1 Can you change it? Read and circle.

1 You _____ change matter.
   (a) can   b can't

2 Water _____ always a liquid.
   a is   b isn't

3 You _____ change the shape of a liquid.
   a can   b can't

4 You _____ change the volume of a liquid.
   a can   b can't

5 The container _____ the volume of the water.
   a changes   b doesn't change

2 Different changes in water. Read and circle.

Water is (1) _____. It can change. It can be a solid, a liquid, or a gas. When it's a liquid, you can change its shape. It takes the shape of its container. You can't change its (2) _____. You can freeze the liquid to make a solid. This solid is called (3) _____. You can (4) _____ the liquid to make a gas. The water changes into (5) _____.

1 a always solid   b always liquid   **(c) matter**
2 a volume   b mixture   c water vapor
3 a water vapor   b ice   c volume
4 a boil   b melt   c freeze
5 a ice   b matter   c water vapor

70 Unit 8

3 Look at the title and the photo, and read the text quickly. What's the text about?

_____

Reading Tip

You don't need to read the whole of the text to understand what it's about. Look at the photo, read the title, and read the text quickly to get an understanding.

My Favorite Place

My favorite place is our holiday house in Sweden. We go there on vacation in the winter and in the summer, and we do very different activities.

A In the winter, the water in the lake freezes. It turns to ice. I go skating on the lake with my sister. The temperature is below 0 °C. Water freezes at 0 °C.

B We drink hot drinks. My dad heats cold water, and the water boils and changes into water vapor. Water vapor is inside the bubbles of boiling water.

C In the spring, the weather is warm, and the ice on the lake melts.

D In the summer, I like drinking cold water. Tiny drops of water form on the glass. Dad says the water vapor in the air touches the cold glass and turns to liquid.

4 Changing states of matter. Look at 3. Read and write A–D.

1 Water changes from a solid to a liquid.   **C**

2 Water changes from a liquid to a gas.   ☐

3 Water changes from a liquid to a solid.   ☐

4 Water changes from a gas to a liquid.   ☐

5 Look, read, and write.

In the summer, I put ice in my lemonade. It's easy to make ice. You ___freeze___ water. The water changes from _____ _____. When you put the ice in your lemonade, the ice _____. It changes from _____.

Unit 8 71

Unit 9 Energy, Motion, and Force

How do energy and forces make objects move?

1 What do the photos show? Write *loud noise* or *soft noise*.

1. loud noise
2. _____
3. _____
4. _____

5. _____
6. _____
7. _____
8. _____

2 Read and write.

| loud noise | force | ~~loud noise~~ | soft noise |

1 A thunderstorm makes a ___loud noise.___

2 A bird makes a _____.

3 It takes a lot of _____ to move a train.

4 A tornado makes a _____.

72 Unit 9

3 Who is using a lot of force? Read and write.

brother   father   ~~grandfather~~
baby brother   mom

Reading Tip

Read the text and think about which actions need a little force or a lot of force.

Ruth: Hi, Tom. What are you doing today?

Tom: Hi, Ruth. We're moving. My father and brother are moving the sofa into the living room. My grandfather is moving the DVD player. My baby brother is moving his toy train. My mom is putting away the dishes.

A Little Force

grandfather
_____
_____

A Lot of Force

_____
_____

4 Look and write.

1 _I push a shopping cart._
   It uses a lot of force.

2 _____
   _____

5 What do you do that uses a little force and a lot of force? What do you do that makes a little noise and a lot of noise? Complete for you.

1 I _____walk to school._____ It uses _____a little_____ force.

2 I _____. It makes _____ noise.

3 _____

4 _____

Unit 9   73

Lesson 1 • What is sound?

1 Facts about sound. Read and match.

1 When an object vibrates,　　　　a a form of energy.

2 Sound is　　　　b how high or low a sound is.

3 Volume is　　　　c it makes a sound.

4 *Pitch* is a word to describe　　　　d how loud or soft a sound is.

2 Let's make some sounds! Read and circle.

Do you want to play an instrument? Play in our SAMBA BAND!

Learn how to hit the drum. Hit it hard, and it (**1**) sounds / **vibrates** strongly to make a loud (**2**) sound / volume. Tap the drum, and it (**3**) sounds / vibrates weakly to make a soft (**4**) pitch / sound.

We are a band of 30 people. We practice every Wednesday night from 5 P.M. to 8 P.M. at St Mark's Primary School.

Remember! We make a lot of noise. If you like high (**5**) volume / sound, come and join us!

3 Look at 2. Read and write.

1 You can learn to play the ___drums___ every Wednesday.

2 The drums are the only _____ in the band.

3 When the drum _____ weakly, the _____ is very soft.

4 When you hit the drum hard, it makes a _____ sound.

74　Unit 9

4 Pitch and volume. Read and choose.

Grammar Tip
An object that vibrates **quickly** makes a sound with a high pitch.
An object that vibrates **slowly** makes a sound with a low pitch.
He hits the drum very **hard**.

Musical Instruments

When you play the Spanish guitar, you can change the pitch. The pitch is high when I pluck the strings and they vibrate (**1**) _b_. The pitch is low when I pluck the strings and they vibrate (**2**) ___.
I also like to play the cymbal. When I hit it very (**3**) ___, it vibrates strongly and the volume is high. When I hit it lightly, it vibrates (**4**) ___ and the volume is low.

1
 a slowly
 b quickly
 c hard

2
 a forcefully
 b quickly
 c slowly

3
 a slowly
 b nicely
 c hard

4
 a weakly
 b slowly
 c hard

5 Can these instruments have a high pitch, a low pitch, or both? Look and circle.

1. high / (low) pitch
2. high / low pitch
3. high / low pitch
4. high / low pitch

6 Choose a musical instrument. Write about its pitch or its volume.

When you play the _____

_____

_____

_____.

Unit 9 75

Lesson 2 • What are motion and force?

1 Facts about motion and force. Read and write.

> zigzag   back and forth   push   pull
> motion   ~~force~~   around and around

1 You make things move with _____*force.*_____

2 _____ is the act of moving.

3 When you move an object one way and then another way, it's called a _____.

4 You _____ an object away from you.

5 You _____ an object toward you.

6 A swing moves _____.

7 The blades of a fan move _____.

2 What can you see in the photos? Look and write *Yes* or *No*.

1 Are the children pushing?   *No*

2 Are the children in motion?   ___

3 Is the boy pulling the ball toward him?   ___

4 Do you need a little force to move this?   ___

5 Is the snake moving in a zigzag?   ___

76 Unit 9

3 Forces and movement in sports. Read and write *away* or *toward*.

Grammar Tip

Someone kicks you a ball. The ball moves **toward** you. You kick it back. The ball moves **away** from you.

A Laura and Jill are throwing and catching a ball. Laura is pushing the ball (**1**) ___away___ from her. She is using force. The ball is moving in a curve. Jill is pulling it (**2**) _____ her.

B Jenny and Sam are playing soccer. Jenny is kicking the ball (**3**) _____ from her. The ball is moving in a straight line.

C Peter is playing baseball. He is throwing the ball. He is pushing it (**4**) _____ from him. The ball is moving in a curve.

D Annabel is skating (**5**) _____ her friends. She is skating in a zigzag.

4 Look and match the photos with *A–D* in **3**.

1. B
2.
3.
4.

5 Imagine you are playing a sport with your friends. Write about what you are all doing.

Today, I am playing _____ with my friends. _____

_____

_____

_____

Unit 9   77

Lesson 3 · What are magnets?

1 An experiment to test what materials a magnet attracts. Read and write.

> ~~attracts~~   attracting   repelling   pole
> repel   attract   magnet

What materials does a magnet attract?
Hypothesis: I predict a magnet (**1**) _attracts_ some metal objects.
Experiment: I use a (**2**) _____ to try to attract objects of different materials. When the magnet pulls an object toward it, it is (**3**) _____ the object. When the magnet pushes an object away from it, it is (**4**) _____ the object. Sometimes the magnet doesn't (**5**) _____ or (**6**) _____ an object. A (**7**) _____ is the place on a magnet that has the strongest push or pull.

2 What objects does a magnet attract? Read and mark (✓) or (✗).

Results:
1. a plastic ruler — ✗
2. a glass bottle — ☐
3. a metal spoon — ☐
4. a fleece jacket — ☐
5. a rubber boot — ☐
6. a book — ☐

3 What is the conclusion of the experiment? Look at 2. Circle and write.

Conclusion: The hypothesis is (**1**) **correct** / **incorrect**. A magnet (**2**) _____.

78   Unit 9

4 Attracting and repelling. Look and write.

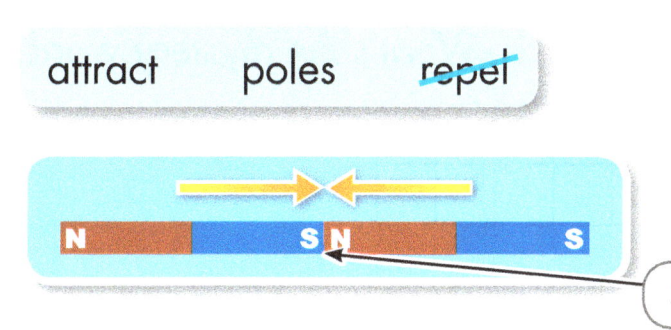

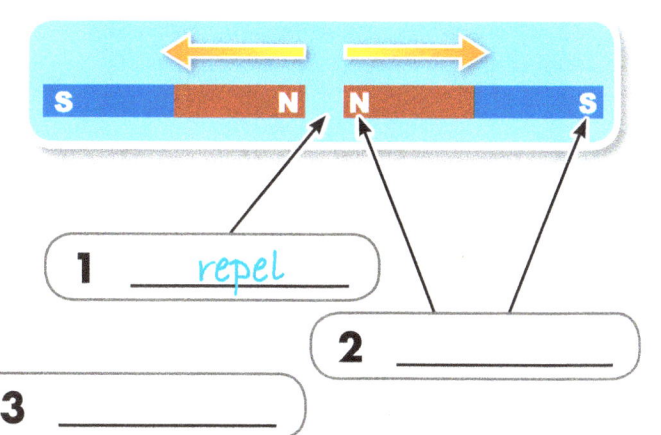

attract   poles   ~~repel~~

1 __repel__

2 _____

3 _____

5 Does a magnet attract or repel another magnet? Read and circle.

Reading Tip
Read all the text before you decide on your answers. There could be some clues further on to help you.

Hypothesis: I predict that one magnet can both repel and attract another.

Experiment: A magnet has (**a**) (two) / three poles. There is a (**b**) west / **north** pole and a (**c**) **south** / east pole.

1 I put the two magnets together and put the (**d**) opposite / **like** poles together. I put a south pole next to another south pole.

2 I put the magnets together and put the (**e**) **opposite** / like poles together. I put a north pole next to a south pole.

6 Look at 5. Number 1 or 2, and write *attract* or *repel*.

Results: ☐ N S + N S = _____

1 N S + S N = _____

7 Can one magnet both repel and attract another? Look at 6. Circle and write.

Conclusion: The hypothesis is (**1**) correct / incorrect. A magnet (**2**) _____.

Unit 9   79

Review 7–9

1 **Look at the photos and write the words. What's the mystery word?**

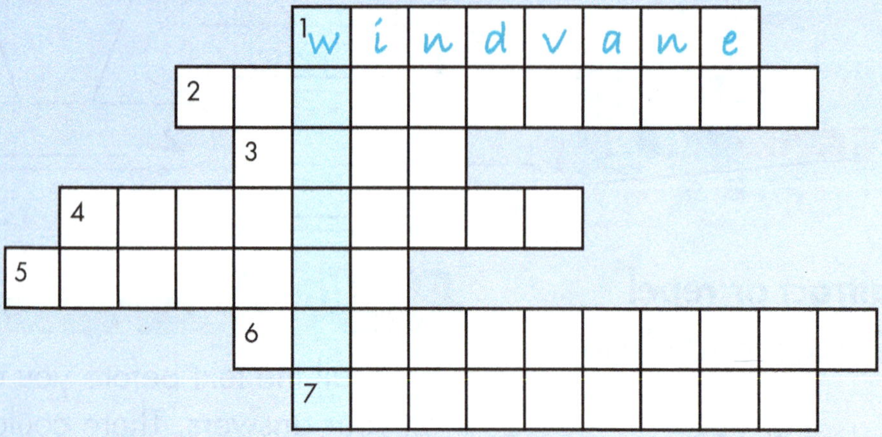

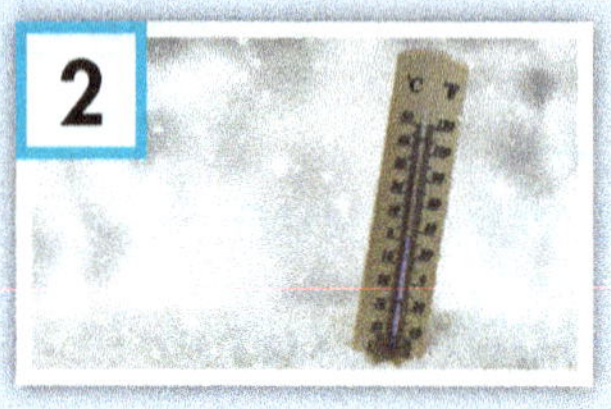

2 **What am I? Complete the words.**

1 I am solid, liquid, or gas. s t a t e of m a t t e r

2 You make bread out of me. d _ _ _ _ _

3 I can be loud or soft. n _ _ _ _

4 I am north or south on a magnet. p _ _ _

5 I measure the speed of the wind. a _ _ _ _ _ _ _ _ _

6 I am made up of two or more kinds of matter. m _ _ _ _ _ _

3 **Circle the odd one out.**

1 **a** precipitation **b** snow **c** sleet **(d)** windy
2 **a** volume **b** evaporate **c** pitch **d** sound
3 **a** lightning **b** drought **c** thunderstorm **d** thunder
4 **a** force **b** push **c** volume **d** pull
5 **a** zigzag **b** back and forth **c** curve **d** gas
6 **a** liquid **b** motion **c** solid **d** gas

4 **Mark (✓) the correct sentences and mark (✗) the incorrect sentences.**

1 **a** Hail falls more forcefully than sleet. ✓
   b Hail falls more softly than sleet. ✗
2 **a** A solid never keeps its own size and shape.
   b A solid always keeps its own size and shape.
3 **a** When guitar strings vibrate quickly, the pitch is low.
   b When guitar strings vibrate quickly, the pitch is high.
4 **a** You pull a shopping cart away from you.
   b You push a shopping cart away from you.
5 **a** You can change the shape of a liquid.
   b You can't change the shape of a liquid.
6 **a** When you hit a cymbal hard, it vibrates strongly.
   b When you hit a cymbal hard, it vibrates weakly.

Vocabulary

Units 1–9 • What do I know?

Which words do you want to remember? Write.

Unit 1

Unit 2

Unit 3

Unit 4

Unit 5

Unit 6

Unit 7 _____

Unit 8 _____

Unit 9 _____

Units 1–9 • What do I know?

I can read and write words about …   ✓   ✗

Unit 1 the nature of science ☐ ☐

Unit 2 technology and tools ☐ ☐

Unit 3 plants and animals ☐ ☐

Unit 4 body and growth ☐ ☐

Unit 5 Earth's materials ☐ ☐

Unit 6 the solar system ☐ ☐

Unit 7 weather ☐ ☐

Unit 8 matter ☐ ☐

Unit 9 energy, motion, and force ☐ ☐

Reading Skills

Units 1–4 • What do I know?

Unit 1   I can look at a table and extract information quickly. ☐

Rock	Weight	Rock	Weight
Granite	400 g	Pumice	200 g

1 Which rock is 400 g? _____
2 Which rock is 200 g? _____

Unit 2   I can read a text and complete it with words from a word pool. ☐

move   shovels   saw

Posted: September 15

I am helping my dad clean up the shed. There are two (1) _____. We use them to (2) _____ the snow in winter. There's a (3) _____, too.

Unit 3   I can scan a text for information. ☐

Which animals use their body parts to get what they need?
Read and circle.

- A pelican has a big beak. It scoops up fish with it.
- A squirrel uses its claws to climb trees to get food.

Unit 4   I can read a paragraph and underline the key words. ☐

Exercise helps to build healthy muscles and joints. It helps you keep a healthy body weight and makes you feel good.

Units 5–9 · What do I know?

Unit 5 I can read the title and look at the photo to understand the gist of a text.

What is the text about? Circle the correct answer.

What can we do?

a things we can do to stop pollution

b things we can do to find clean water

Unit 6 I can read a text and complete a table.

Jupiter is planet number five from the sun. Its orbit takes 12 years. Saturn's orbit takes 29 years. It is planet number six.

Name	(a)	Saturn
Planet Number	5	6
Orbit (Years)	12	(b)

Unit 7 I can read and identify words with similar meanings.
Read and match.

1 precipitation   a bad

2 severe   b rain

Unit 8 I can use a picture to help understand a text.
Look, read, and circle.

At 100 °C, (1) water vapor / water changes to (2) a liquid / water vapor.

Unit 9 I can read and understand what needs a little force or a lot of force.

Read and circle.

1 lift a feather   a little / a lot

2 kick a ball hard   a little / a lot

Reading Skills 85

Writing Skills

Units 1–4 • What do I know?

Unit 1 I can write the results of an experiment. ☐

Which box has both a lot of red apples and a lot of green apples?

	Box A	Box B	Box C
Red apples	3	5	10
Green apples	4	12	10

Answer: _____

Unit 2 I can write simple sentences about what I do. ☐

When it's snowing, I _____.

When it's windy, I _____.

Unit 3 I can use notes to write about an animal. ☐

The Horned Lizard
Habitat: forests
Stays safe: horns, body gets bigger, horns stick out

The horned lizard lives _____
_____
_____.

Unit 4 I can use information to complete a text. ☐

Adolescents: 10 hours a night, 2,800 calories a day, 420 minutes a week

Adolescents need to sleep **(1)** _____.
They need to eat **(2)** _____. They need to exercise **(3)** _____.

86 Writing Skills

Units 5–9 · What do I know?

Unit 5 I can write a list.

How can you help protect Earth? Look at page 45 of your Workbook for ideas and write.

_____

_____

Unit 6 I can complete a text about a picture.

This is Ursa Major. It's a group of stars called a (**1**) _____. It (**2**) _____ a bear.

Unit 7 I can complete a text by reading symbols on a weather map.

In Paris, it's there's (**1**) _____.
In Lyon, there's (**2**) _____.
In Nice, it's (**3**) _____.

Unit 8 I can complete a table correctly.

State of Matter	Keeps Its Own Shape Y / N	Takes the Shape of the Container Y / N
Milk	(**1**)	(**2**)	(**3**)

Unit 9 I can label pictures with scientific information.

Write *push away* or *pull toward*.

_____   _____

Writing Skills **87**

Study Skills

Learning science words

- Record new words in your notebook.

- Write whether the new word is a verb, noun, adjective, or adverb.

- Write a sentence that includes the new word. This helps you remember how the word is used and what it means.

- Group new words by topic. Use the words when you write about that topic.

Carrying out research

- Think carefully about what you want to find out.

- You can do a simple hands-on experiment.

- You can find people who know about the topic, and ask them questions.

- You can look for information on websites, in magazines or in books.

Using visual guides

- Use mind maps to show how ideas are connected. Put the central idea in a circle in the middle. Draw more circles, and draw lines to connect these to the middle circle. Write connected ideas in these circles.

- Use bar charts to record information. For example, you can record the results of your class's favorite colors. Write the number of students on the vertical axis and different colors on the horizontal axis. Complete the bar chart with the correct number of students for each color.